CAST YOURSELF

The Actor's Guide to Self-Producing

by

KATHI CAREY

Carey-it-Off Publishing
Los Angeles, California

Cast Yourself: The Actor's Guide to Self-Producing
© 2019 by Kathi Carey
First Edition

All rights reserved. No part of this book may be reproduced or transmitted in any form or by any means, electronic or mechanical, including photocopying, recording, or by any information storage and retrieval system, without written permission from the author, except for the inclusion of brief quotations in a review. Inquiries should be addressed to:

Carey-it-Off Publishing
5152 Sepulveda #205
Sherman Oaks, California 91403
818.789.0954
publisher@carey-it-off.com
carey-it-off.com

Cover Design by Kim Courtright

ISBN 978-0-578-56754-9

What Others Are Saying About Cast Yourself and Kathi's Self-Producing Seminars

"What I learned from Kathi was practical advice about how to begin by first making a list of what might be available to me to use during shooting -- Locations, crew and donations.

"When I started proceeding like that, I saw I had resources I hadn't thought about. I got excited and thought wow, I guess I can try to produce a web series.

"We wrote, produced, shot and made a lot of mistakes. Without Kathi's initial 'self-producing hints' I would have never had the nerve to move ahead and actually do it. Next time, I will get a better team to shoot my series. Each time you learn more.

"I'm an acting coach and have passed on so much of Kathi's self-producing information to the actors who study with me. It has helped several I know become SAG-AFTRA eligible. Actors feel so much more empowered when they know they can give themselves a place to act. Kathi's experience and information will help you earn your producer hat. Go for it."

---Judy Kerr, author, coach

"Don't even think about starting your project until you read Kathi's book - her information is invaluable to both the novice and the seasoned self-producer. The time and money you will save if you follow her lead is indescribable."

---Michelle Eagle-Wolfe, actress

"I had the opportunity to hear Kathi's presentation on self-producing and let me tell you, she knows her stuff. Any questions I may have had she answered in complete detail. She told me what forms I needed, exactly what to ask for, where to go. She has done her research and knows what she's talking about. When you decide to self-produce make sure you make your life simple, read Kathi's book, *The Actor's Guide to Self Producing*. It will save you from a lot of headaches."

---Janean Jeffries, actress

"Kathi Carey is a consummate professional, and a perfect example of an actor-producer extraordinaire who has taken her career into her own hands. She understands how to create brilliant art on a budget, and do so in a way that respects everyone involved. If every set were run the way Kathi runs hers, this industry would be a much better place."

---Ben Whitehair, actor, social media expert

"Hearing Kathi's advice on self-producing not only made it seem a whole lot less intimidating but made me realize that I was making things WAY too hard on myself! Her information is useful, practical and totally empowering."

---Mandi Moss, actress

"Kathi Carey was a self-producer before the web made it cool. From blank page to red-carpet premiere, Kathi is an expert on every part of the self-producing process. Kathi offers powerful and practical insights on how to produce properly, cheaply, and effectively. Kathi not only helped me figure out HOW to create my web series, *Napoleon Bon Appétit*, but her words INSPIRED me to self-produce in the first place."

---Derek Houck, actor, producer, Napoleon Bon Appétit

"I'd never really thought about Self-Producing. It was an intimidating thought as I didn't really know how to even begin producing something. Kathi was awesome. She went through every part of self-producing like it was nobody's business. :) From writing the piece, to locations, to what kind of crew you're gonna need. I definitely came out with SO much knowledge, I feel like I can for sure create something great that I wouldn't have known how to before."

---Tash Phillips, actress, singer

"Kathi Carey considers every speed bump that comes along with self-producing and makes it easy to navigate for yourself. I'm thankful to know Kathi, and I've used her "list of assets" secret for every film I've produced. A little research goes a long way in producing, and you've picked up the right book."

---Amber Rose Plaster, actor/producer

"Kathi Carey knows how to self-produce successfully. Kathi is an industry gem of generosity, helping other actors who desire to follow her lead and inspiring them to do so. After learning about self-producing from Kathi I thought, 'I want to I will...The rest is up to me, because Kathi has shown me the professional way to self-produce!' Thank you Kathi!"

"Kathi shares her professional 'inside knowledge' on self producing so that it is not overwhelming--it is exciting. I know prior to learning from Kathi, I thought to myself, as many actors do, 'Self producing is too complicated.' Well, Kathi will simplify it for you. She taught me that not only was it _more_ than doable, as an actor, to self-produce, but also the importance of doing it professionally. I am inspired to self-produce my own content and will do it with CONFIDENCE due to Kathi sharing her knowledge on the topic."

---*Cait Mathis, actress*

"Kathi has a distinct eye for clarity in finding an actor's unique gifts and setting a game plan in motion to showcase those talents. In very realistic terms, Kathi helps actors to formulate a course of action to create self-produced content that is at once doable, interesting and most importantly actor-brand specific and tells The Industry exactly how to use the actor in the future."

---*Ben Hensley, actor*

"With the film business being extremely cutthroat, it is nice to have people who genuinely care for your success. Kathi is extremely knowledgeable in all aspects of the business and takes the time to help point whomever she is helping in the right direction."

---*Ryan Jarrell, actor*

"Kathi's knowledge of self-producing seems endless! She is a true self-made success, and proves that with dedication and hard work, talent can be channeled to accomplish great things. A real inspiration!"

---*Jacqueline Gardner, actress/producer*

"I met Kathi Carey in Bonnie Gillespie's Self-Management for Actors class, and she had a full day of class to discuss self-producing. Even in that full day, Kathi was only able to dispense a sliver of her incredible knowledge, but her passion and expertise were clear. She shined a light on so many things that I never knew went into self-producing and I walked away that day with a Word document chock-full of notes as well as a brain teeming with extremely valuable information. Through this foundation of inspiration, I am now in pre-production for my first film as a writer, producer, and actor in an on-brand role. If I hadn't met (and listened to!) Kathi Carey, there is no way I would know how to even begin this exciting self-producing process. She knows what she's doing and her passion will inspire you to be awesome on this journey too!"

--*Anne Woods, actress/writer/producer*

You got a dream, you gotta protect it.
People can't do somethin' themselves,
they wanna tell you you can't do it.
If you want somethin', go get it. Period.
— The Pursuit of Happyness, 2006
Gabriele Muccino, dir.

This book is dedicated to
all the actors
who are pursuing their
dreams by creating content,
one project at a time.

*This is nothing! Piece of cake! Producing is
being a samurai warrior.
They pay you day in, day out for years so
that one day, when called upon,
you can respond, your training at its peak,
and save the day!*
— Wag the Dog, 1997
Barry Levinson, dir.

Table of Contents

Foreword	iii
Introduction	v
Acknowledgements	vii
Part One: Approach	**1**
1: Who am I? Or Who Are You?	3
2: Why, Oh Why?	9
3: With a Little Help From My Friends	15
4. Nuts and Bolts	21
5: Yikes!! Producing Isn't Free	27
Part Two: Pre-Production	**33**
6: Your Team	35
7: Union, Permits, Insurance	43
8: Scheduling	47
9: Script Breakdown	51
Part Three: Production	**57**
10: Final Checklist	59
Part Four: Post-Production	**65**
11: On the Cutting Room Floor	67
12: The Score	73
13: Sound and Sound FX	77
14: Color Correction	81
15: The Mix	85
Part Five: Distribution	**91**
16: Marketing	93
17: Distribution Outlets	97
18: So Who's Going to See It?	109

19: New Technologies   115

Part Six: Industry Recognition   119
20: Something Gold and Shiny   121

Part Seven: Closing Words of Wisdom   129
21: Do's and Don'ts Or Nuggets of Information   131
22: The End is Really the Beginning   137

Appendix   139
i. Positions and Definitions   141
ii. Film Festival Information   165
iii. Selected Reading   171
iv. Sample Press Releases   175
v. Glossary of Terms   183
End Notes   187

Foreword

"You want to make something of yourself? *Make* something yourself." – Dom Hughes, Rockwood Films

Once upon a time, actors who did anything other than acting were not taken seriously. Today, if you "only" act, the big question is, "Really? That's all you've got?"

There's a revolution afoot, and Kathi Carey is unquestionably at the forefront. Folks who create their own content, who build their marketable brand via self-produced footage, and who cultivate a fanbase without the assistance of some big "power agent" are leading the field today. What a wonderful time to be in this delicious business of ours!

When I first started teaching actors how to empower themselves using the *Self-Management for Actors* principles, Kathi was quick to share her journey as a content creator. Not one to wait for anything to become trendy, Kathi was very early to the party that is now dominated by award-winning self-producing ninjas.

Here's why that should be important to you: Kathi has not only the ability to walk you through your journey as a potentially award-winning content creator; she can spot trends about where self-producing is going within our beloved industry. She can lead you to the next tier, if you're open to doing a ridiculous amount of hard work.

Yeah. Sorry. I'm not going to sugarcoat it. Creating your own content is not for the hobbyists. It's not for the weak of heart. It's not for the results-oriented creative folks out there. It's for you, the future of Hollywood. It's for you, the leader in your market. It's for you, the person who knows that storytelling at the highest level is no longer a closed loop — it's one you can be a part of, if you're willing to do the work.

In CAST YOURSELF, *The Actor's Guide to Self-Producing*, Kathi leads you through the process of self-producing. She shares her decades of experience (and success) so that you can get to building your experience (and success) too.

As you dive in, here, remember that your journey is your own. Your experiences may not look like those your peers have. You are your own best brand manager. And the biggest gift you can give yourself is investing in yourself, because if you're not your own biggest fan, how can you expect anyone else to be?

Think about what inspired you to be an actor. You wanted to tell stories. Those stories are within your control. You get to show the world what your craft can help articulate, every day. You just have to be ready to do the work. Thank goodness Kathi is here to walk us through that process!

--Bonnie Gillespie
author, casting director, producer

Introduction

Those who know me will recall that I founded a repertory company for film and television in Los Angeles and supervised its activities for about twenty years. We were an unlikely mix of the old Hollywood studio system and a band of renegade, guerrilla filmmakers showing respect only to our fellow artists and the audiences destined to see our work. We would take in actors, brand and train them and school them in many things beyond acting technique—like a finishing school, if you will—and handle their PR. It could be said that we instructed our members in a unique acting technique which included the ability to find and create work as an integral part of that technique.

As the repertory company grew, some of the actors took on greater responsibility and undertook the training and management of actors coming into the group. This meant using writing, directing, and marketing skills to the benefit of others as well as themselves. The first to do so, and with stellar results, was Kathi Carey.

Kathi had a very complete understanding of her personal brand as an actress (though I referred to it as 'signature', a term I brought back with me from France after beginning my film career there). Branding was not the high profile topic then that it has become in recent times, but it was obvious to me that the studios of old took it seriously and it was a foundational aspect of life in the repertory company. Kathi carried this understanding into her activities as a writer/director and created films that consistently reward the viewer with her perspective, intellect and aesthetic wavelength.

What I admire most about Kathi is that she has never stopped learning about the film industry and she puts her knowledge into action making films from her own blueprint, sending her own message delivering memorable films to the screen.

This book is invaluable to actors, writers and directors who rebel at having to ask permission to practice their art. It is written by someone who knows the terrain and is navigating it well and with style. Kathi's message is not do as I say but, rather, do as I do. I wish I had access to such a book when I was starting out.

--Stephen Mitchell
writer/producer/director and author of *Action/Reaction*

Acknowledgements

When I first started on this journey I was, possibly much like you, *just* an actor and really never considered writing, producing or directing. However, luckily I started working with a man who was, admittedly, ahead of his time: Stephen Mitchell. One of the first things we did together was a half-hour, improvised dramatic 30 minute piece, which was taped for local cable that he called "Discussions." When it aired he got a call from Mike Figgis, requesting a copy of the tape so he could study it for a film he was working on—*Internal Affairs*. This was the genesis of thousands of shows, several series and a few films that would be produced over the next several years. At his urging and under his tutelage I learned writing, directing and producing and wrote/directed and produced many of those projects...in fact, well over 1,000.

I hardly know where to begin when creating a list of all the people who have brought me to where I am today in my filmmaking career. Basically, if I hadn't started on a filmmaking career there would be no book. I will attempt to single out some of the people here who have made the biggest impact. Here goes...

First, a BIG thank you to my SFMA (that's Self Management for Actors) family and Team Cricket Feet, headed up by Bonnie Gillespie and Keith Johnson for welcoming me as part of the team and part of the family. They invited me to teach my self-producing principles to hundreds of actors over the years, which was always a joyful experience. I hope I was able to help some of them on their journey of content creation. Also, particularly, to the ninjas who helped facilitate the SMFA class (where I taught): Ryan Basham, Amber Plaster and Jacqueline Steiger... y'all made it fun along the way!

I am so grateful for the mentorship and friendship shown to me from Marvin V. Acuna, Mary Lou Belli, John Cothran, Cassian Elwes, Anita Haeggstrom, Basil Hoffman, Marita Grabiak, Linda Gray, Cathryn Jaymes, Fred Lehne, Brian McNamara, Dean Parisot, Tracy Samuels, Mews Small, James Patrick Stuart, Jason Stuart, Steve Tom, Marc and Elaine Zicree...people who are tiers above me in this business but have all taken the time to assist me in my filmmaking journey.

For all the crew members and cast members of the productions I have been a part of, either as an actress or as a writer, producer or director for showing me how things get done professionally, on-time and on-budget and always with a lot of grace and joy. Y'all don't know this (or maybe you do) but I have been watching and learning from you every time I walk on the set. Particularly David Raiklen, MarLee Candell and Gabriel Diniz who have been with me through many projects and, hopefully, many more.

To the brilliant filmmakers whose work I've shared in quotes throughout this book. Your work inspires me to be a better writer/producer and director and I strive to make this happen each and every day.

To Stephen Mitchell, the one who started it all. I'm not sure what you saw in me, but you pushed me through some initial reluctance into a filmmaking career when all I really wanted to do was act. For that I will be eternally grateful.

And finally, to those closest to my heart...my biggest supporters: Dave Balch who did the yeoman's job of putting this book together, technically, for me; my sweet mother, who continued to teach me things every day I cared for her, even though she never knew I wrote a book; and my husband, David, who challenges me and supports me each day that we spend together. Thank you for being there, for pushing me to be the best 'me' I can be, each and every day of my life.

--Kathi

Acknowledgements — ix

Part One: Approach

All you need is twenty seconds of insane courage and I promise you something great will come of it.

—We Bought a Zoo, 2011
Cameron Crowe, dir

1: Who am I? Or Who Are You?

Before starting your self-producing journey the most important question you need to ask yourself is…"Who am I? What do I represent as a product or as a brand? What's my 'signature?'" When you sign your name on a document, you have a unique way of signing that is yours and yours alone. No one else can sign your name the way you do and that's called your signature. If someone tried to duplicate that *exactly*, we'd call it a forgery. In acting, your signature is your unique essence, what you bring to the 'party' (or the role) that no one else does. The look, feel, voice…all the qualities that are unique to you. Many people in the business call that your "type," your "brand" or your "essence." I'll use all those terms interchangeably.

The better defined a product is, the easier it is to market. We all know that Volvo is the "safest car in the world" and that BMW is the "ultimate driving machine" because they've told us so in their advertising. Is it any wonder, then, that you see a lot of moms with car seats driving Volvos and younger up-and-comers who are trying to impress driving BMWs? Never mind that if you've ever driven a Porsche or a Ferrari you might dispute BMW's claim of "ultimate driving machine" (LOL!).

The Studio System of Old Hollywood knew how to 'brand' actors and did it brilliantly. They had a whole system whereby actors would be trained — given classes in diction, movement, acting, singing, etc. — in order to prepare them for the roles they would inhabit in the studios' films. Looking back you can see how well it was done. There was the 'plucky girl next door,' the 'man's man,' the 'vixen,' the 'romantic leading man,' the ingénue,' the 'tough guy,' and on and on. Now, actors are on their own and today the buzzword on everyone's lips is "branding." All it really means is that you, the actor, need to have a well defined, unique something that can be seen and described (in a few words or a phrase) so that people know, instantly, how to cast you.

How do you figure out what your 'brand' is or how do you get one? I'll let you in on a little secret—you already have one. You just may not know it yet. All you need to do is discover what it is. However, it's not necessarily easy to discover in oneself for two reasons: first, because we often have a difficult time looking objectively at ourselves and second, because we know everything there is to know about ourselves. We know our entire history. So yes, on the outside you may look and sound like the creepy bad guy, but you know that inside you're just the nicest guy in the world. Getting to the point where you realize that playing creepy bad guys is FUN and you can make tons of money doing just that is the key.

I'm not going to tell you how to figure out what your brand or signature is because there are some great coaches out there who do an excellent job of helping you discover that. Bonnie Gillespie has a book, *Self-Management for Actors* as well as online tools and courses designed to help you figure out *exactly* what your brand is. Stephen Mitchell does online coaching in branding and brand-management for actors and other artists and I'm sure there are others as well.

What you need to know is that those qualities that make you uniquely you—those things that set you apart from everyone else on planet Earth—those are the very things that make your friends like you and they are also the things that will draw an audience to you. So, finding your brand will be a little bit discovery of who you are, a little bit finding out how you appear to the world—what you present when you walk in a room—and a LOT of looking objectively at how you've been cast before. This means figuring out what those qualities are that have been present in every character you've played, even characters that seem diametrically opposed. You may even find yourself surveying random people to find out what they see: do people see you as the "good ol' gal?" or the "rich socialite?" Are you the "smooth as silk" leading man or the "geeky side-kick?" Are you "techno-phobic" or "techno-savvy?" Are you "Casper Milquetoast?" or the "biggest bad-ass" who ever walked the face of the earth? What do people see when they first meet you? As you get into the process you may find that this is actually fun!

If you've never thought about this before you *may* be thinking to yourself "But Kathi, I don't want to get typecast!" Umm...yeah, you do. However, probably not in the way you're thinking. When you're first starting out in your career, before you're a big star and a household name, it's so much easier for those who are hiring you if they know what they're hiring before they do so. It's just like when you go to the grocery store—do you automatically reach for the plain-wrap, generic brand cereal? No. You have a *brand* that you prefer. If I were to ask you to name ketchup what's the first name that comes to mind? Some no-name, store-brand, generic catsup? No. It would be Heinz, of course. Why? Because they have branded themselves into your consciousness. I'm going to tell you a little secret – the brand name and the plain-wrap are often made at the same factory. But more people reach for the brand name. Why? Marketing. People are *aware* of the brand name. People *want* the brand name.

You *want* to become a brand name. By being specific in your marketing—honing in on what makes you special—you stand out from the crowd and you are no longer a plain-wrap actor in a sea of plain-wrap actors. Once you're well known you can branch out and show the business (and the world) all the various colors and variety of characters you're capable of playing *besides* the more narrow confines of your brand. But for now, in order to get IN and create that brand awareness, you need to present a well-defined brand.

It is vitally important that this step come first. DO NOT go forward into content creation until this step is completed.

Why? Because every step in self-producing that comes after this hinges on this step. You cannot start looking for or developing material to produce until you know what your brand is because you're going to be developing material that showcases—what else? *That brand.* Why waste time and money producing a project for yourself as a romantic leading woman when what you *really* play is the nosy girl-next-door? You won't be presenting *your* brand *and* the buyers won't respond so you'll just be wasting your time and money.

Let me stress this again: Please, please, *please* don't spend a fortune producing a project for yourself as the romantic leading man (or woman) if that's clearly *not* your brand. If your brand is a character—produce a project for *that* brand. Better to have a project that sells *you*, exactly as you need and want to be sold to your buyers, than to have a project that sells you in a way you have never *been* and would never *be* hired. It doesn't do you any good to have off-brand footage on your reel or to have people see it.

Let me give you an example: I was at a film festival and saw a feature that a young woman had written and produced for herself, in which she was the star as a romantic leading-lady. It was a romantic comedy and, you guessed it, it wasn't right for her. She would have been better cast as the quirky, geeky best friend. Due to the fact that she was miscast, the response to the film was tepid at best. I knew she'd never sell the film nor make her investors their money back. It was sad, really, because she did a good job, was a good actress and it was great material – the film was just off-brand for her and, as a result, the whole thing felt wrong and the audience response was flat.

I'm going to repeat this, because I have seen it happen over and over, in projects large and small: When someone starts to produce something *for themselves* they suddenly decide that NOW they have the chance to play that role they've always wanted to play (in which they've never been and never would be cast). The problem is that the role is something so off-brand that *of course* they've never been and never would be cast that way, so they end up wasting a lot of time and money on a project that, ultimately, never goes anywhere or does anything for them. Just because you want something to be your brand doesn't mean it IS your brand. Hopefully, by now you're saying, "Hey Kathi—I get it. Move on!"

I'm telling you that you can create a kick-ass project for *any brand*. Period. Look at all the cool, interesting, quirky, unusual actors out there who are working all the time. Christopher Walken comes to mind. So does Steve Buscemi. Dustin Hoffman, Lena Dunham, Rebel Wilson, Mindy Kaling and Kristin Wiig. None of these are classic leading men or women. But they all have created characters that were so on-brand you will never forget them.

All right, Mr. DeMille, I'm ready for my close-up.
—Sunset Boulevard, 1950
Billy Wilder, dir

2: Why, Oh Why?

Having fun yet? Well, I hope so. Hopefully you can see that this is putting you more in control of your destiny as an artist.

Now, before you begin writing or developing your project, you need to ask yourself a couple of questions:

(1) "Why am I doing this?" and

(2) "What do I want to have happen because I did this?"

Why do we ask these questions? Because, you want to be sure that you're producing the right *type* of project to get the results that you want. There are several different kinds of projects out there that you could produce for yourself: a play or theatre piece, a feature film, a short film, a web series or new media project, a one-off web piece or scene or sketch (if you do comedy). There may be other platforms that have come along since the book has been published—but these are the ones that most actors choose from when deciding to self-produce a project as I write this. Each one of these different types of projects will be seen by a different public. Yes, the audience (or public) for these projects may overlap, but primarily they each attract a different viewing public. When you know what you want to accomplish, who you want to see your project or what your end goal is, you can determine which type of project to produce to get the desired results.

Each one of these different types of projects will accomplish a different goal for you. Let's take them one by one.

A Play or Theatre Piece (Live Theatre)

This type of entertainment venue will be seen by the least amount of people for the time and effort involved. That, however, doesn't deter many actors (and should not deter you, if this is your passion). There are those who just love the theatre and don't care whether their efforts are seen by one, 100 or 1,000. I have never produced a theatre piece, although I have directed one, so I won't spend a lot of time telling you the ins and outs of producing for the theatre. I will just say that it's probably as difficult — if not more difficult — than any of the other venues that we will discuss with the least "bang for the buck." This means you'll spend as much or more money — and probably more time — producing your piece and it will be seen by the least amount of people by a factor of 10 (maybe 100). But, if this is the way you want to go, then do some research on the subject, find a good book about producing theatre in your part of the world, go out and find appropriate material and go for it!

A Feature Film/Short Film

I'm going to lump these two together because it's been said that producing a short film requires 90% of the work of a feature, in 10% of the time with 0.3% of the manpower and 0.01% of the budget. Films are usually premiered these days at festivals, distributed through a variety of outlets and formats, including theatres, DVDs, Netflix/VOD, television and cable. A short is considered anything from one minute to 40 minutes (depending on who's doing the defining). A feature is considered anything from 80 minutes to whatever the audience will stand (I've heard of six-hour movies, but two is usually the norm).

Web Series/One-Off (New Media)

We'll lump these two together because the delivery system is the same. Whether it's a series (more than one) or just one (like one scene you put up on Funny or Die[i] or YouTube[ii]), you're putting something up on the web for people to watch on their computer, their handheld mobile devices or tablets. It's all lumped together as "new media" these days.

Why not discuss television, you ask? Because *you* can't self-produce anything that would be *broadcast* (or cablecast) on television, pay cable or even basic cable (like USA, FX, AMC) today. Although you might find that your web series or single episode goes viral and gets "picked up" by a television network or cable station (or even Netflix or Hulu or the like) for development into a series—you can't count on that and you can't go straight from your production to putting it there.

Now we ask the questions again: "Why are you doing this?" and "What do you want to have happen because you did it?" The answer to those two questions will determine just what type of project you will want to produce and how you will go about doing so.

If what you really want is a scene or two for your reel, you probably only want to do a scene or two. That sounds obvious, right? But you'd be surprised at how many people just want a scene or two for their reel and decide they need to produce a short film, an entire web series with 15 episodes or even a feature in order to accomplish this.

If you just want a scene or two for your reel, you just need to produce a little sketch or a couple of sketches to put up on a web channel (like *Funny or Die*) or create your own YouTube channel and put them there (we'll discuss distribution outlets in Chapter 17) or, in fact, just put whatever you produce *on your reel*. You see, it doesn't necessarily need to go anywhere if what you want is something punchy and on-brand for your reel.

However, if what you want is to prove that you can carry a sitcom, then you might want to produce an entire first season of a comedy web series where you would play the lead

Why, O Why? — 11

or one of the main characters in an ensemble. That would accomplish the goal of showing you carrying the show, or sharing the show with several others, in a comedy setting. If you're able to create some buzz and the show is funny, there's no telling what kind of attention you might be able to attract. The least you'll be able to do is get some good material for your reel to show that you should *be* on a sitcom. The same is true for drama—there are some great drama web series out there getting a lot of buzz these days and there's no reason you can't produce your own multi-episode new media project in the drama, sci fi or even action genre. Any of these could also help you if you're interested in joining the Television Academy or putting yourself up in the FYC. (More on that in Chapter 20.) Anything goes, right? The key is to decide what fits your brand.

If you want to show that you can carry a feature or be the "bad guy," or the "femme fatale," or any character, really, in a feature without taking the time, or spending the money, to actually make a feature, then a short film is your ticket. It can be done relatively inexpensively (compared with the cost of a feature) in as short as a day or two, or as long as a week or more. When we get to the chapter on delivery and distribution, I'll discuss how to get these projects out into the marketplace in the best way possible. Right now we're deciding what type of project to do. The same thing goes here, as well, if you're interested in the possibility of going for a nomination for an Academy Award. I'll show you how to go about doing that with a short film in Chapter 20.

If you definitely want to do a feature, go for it. All I will say about that is you are going to have a fairly substantial 'ramp up,' meaning it could take as little as six to nine months and as long as two to five years to get it financed and shot, and then another one to three years to get it through post and out into the marketplace. Trust me on this. You first have to come up with a brilliant idea and then you (or someone you know) has to write the screenplay. Writing a good screenplay, and then doing the rewrites—and you should count on a minimum of two to four rewrites—will take you at least a year, if you're pretty fast. It *could* take you a year just to write the first draft. Once you've got a draft you're happy with, then you have to raise the money. This is a process that is totally dependent upon who you're working with and how much money you're trying to raise. Beyond that, you have to schedule pre-production (which is usually at least twice what your production window will be), production and post-production. So, say your production window is 6 weeks—that means your pre-production should be 12 weeks, followed by 6 weeks of production. After that you'll need six to nine months of post-production. So, your whole pre-to-post time frame is a year-long process! Can you see now why people opt to do a short film for their first, second and sometimes even third projects?

I was asked by an actor to create a project for him that would show that he could carry a feature *and* that he could speak with both a British accent and an American accent, all with the brand of a charming, charismatic, no-bullshit action hero with a conscience. Well, there wasn't enough budget to produce a feature film, but I wrote a kick-ass short film that showed him speaking with both his British and American accents, a couple of action sequences, a chase, a fight, an explosion and, of course, his wry sense of humor and charm. Oh, and he wanted to show that he was capable of working with series regular-level actors so that those meetings he was having at higher-level agencies and management companies would pay off. We cast him opposite Golden Globe-nominee Brian McNamara[iii] (who, at the time I shot the film, was starring in Lifetime's *Army Wives*) and Basil Hoffman[iv] who had a nice part in the previous year's Academy-Award-winning film *The Artist*.

I am big! It's the pictures that got small.
—Sunset Boulevard, 1950
Billy Wilder, dir.

3: With a Little Help From My Friends

When I teach this class in person, it is at this point where I recommend that the actors a list of their assets. Most of the time the actors look at me like I'm crazy. "We're actors," they say, "we don't have any assets." Yes, I know. As actors we often don't have a lot of money in the bank, savings accounts, 401k accounts, stock portfolios or investments of any kind. However, those aren't necessarily the types of assets to which I'm referring.

Did you ever see the movie *El Mariachi*?[v] It was made for a paltry $7,000. How, you ask? Because Robert Rodriguez utilized his assets. That's right. He figured out what he had access to and then he wrote the script to accommodate those assets. That's what I want you to do.

What? You mean you want me to make a list of stuff and *then* write a script that incorporates all that stuff on the list? Yes. That's exactly what I want you to do.

After you've determined your brand, your unique signature that you're going to use this project to promote, I want you to sit down with a piece of paper and a pen (or a computer and a Word program) and make a list. Write down everything you can think of that you own, that you have access to, that your friends own and that they have access to. This includes knick-knacks, collections, cars, apartments, locations, and random items that don't fit in any category. Don't stop until you've exhausted everything you can think of. This may take several days, because just when you think you're done, you suddenly remember something else, even hours or days later. That's fine. Keep coming back and adding to the list for as long as you need.

Oh, and don't forget about your relationships. Not just your relationships with people. I wrote, produced and directed a project for an actor who was a former competitive athlete. When he sent me his list he neglected to tell me that he had had major corporate sponsorships when he was competing. Had I known about those, the project would've been different by taking advantage of those corporations and their varying products. We won't forget to list those assets for the next project! And if you're asking the question... yes, every actor who comes to me and asks me to create a project for them gets this assignment after, of course, we figure out their branding and their 'why.'

These assets will be the building blocks of your project. Again, please note what I've just said here. I didn't say, "Go write some brilliant script starring Brand You." Nope. I want you to tailor the project to take advantage of all the assets on your list, whether you write the project yourself or you get someone else to write it for you. This is how you will save money throughout your production.

For instance, instead of writing a scene to take place at a mansion in Beverly Hills—which you don't have and would have to try and obtain and pay for—you would write that same scene to take place at a large home in Pasadena (which your friend's parents own and will let you use for a day). Instead of writing that your character drives a Porsche convertible, you'd write that he drives a Toyota, which you already drive, thereby saving yourself the rental and insurance fees for obtaining the Porsche.

If someone is going to write the piece for you or if you are going to co-write the piece with someone else, you will want to have that list of assets handy as you write. As you go from scene to scene, refer to the list in order to decide where to locate the action (locations you already have access to) and what types of props to feature (things you already have or have access to).

Your characters will do things that you or your friends actually DO. For instance, if you work as a bartender and you have access to the bar during the day to shoot a scene (when it's normally closed to the public), then one of your characters could be a bartender, or one of the scenes might take place at that bar. See how that works? If one of your friends teaches piano and gives private lessons to wealthy people and their children, then one of the characters might do that for a living and you could actually use one of the students, their home and piano.

Not only does this save you money as a producer, but it actually makes it easier to write as well. Beginning writers often suffer from what I call "choice overload." In other words—too many choices. As you are writing there are so many places you could set your scenes, so many types of characters you could populate your piece with, so many twists and turns you could write into your piece that, as you go along, you become frozen because there are just too many choices and it's difficult to narrow them down to just one. By making a list of the things you have at your disposal, you narrow your choices of what to write, which makes it easier to write your piece. Also, when you have a specific "type", clearly defined, that you're writing for (your own brand, as well as others in the piece), it helps define your characters as well. By delineating more and more elements of the piece, you'll find it becomes easier, instead of more difficult, to write.

I won't get too much into writing here—but suffice it to say that knowing the qualities embodied in your lead character (your *protagonist*) will make it much easier to know who the antagonist *needs* to be, and the qualities *that* character must possess. Conversely, if your brand demands that you play the antagonist instead of the protagonist (and many do), having that character clearly defined will inform you of the many qualities that the protagonist must exhibit. If your character is the "comedy relief" that, too, will tell you what types of other characters need to populate your piece.

Starting with one clearly defined character will help you define the other characters. I know you're scratching your head and saying to yourself, "Really? It can't be that easy." And no, it's not THAT easy. But trust me on this—it will make it *easier*. I've written thousands of hours of cable shows, feature scripts, shorts and webisodes. Here's what I've found: The more clearly defined your characters—the easier it is to write. The more narrow your choices, in terms of locations, job descriptions, and the like, the easier it is to write. When 'the world is your oyster,' so to speak, in terms of writing, you really can end up staring at the blank page because the choices seem endless and it's difficult to narrow them down to just one.

There are some great resource books regarding writing, structure and so forth in the Appendix. If you want to try your hand at writing I suggest you check some of them out. Additionally, if you're *really* serious about writing, watch good movies, start reading screenplays and start writing… a lot. Every day, if you can. In fact, I subscribe to the recommendation in "The Artist's Way" by Julia Cameron to write what she calls *morning pages* every day. If you really want to be a writer, I would get and read her book and give the morning pages a try. The way to get good at *anything* is to do it.

I have always depended on the kindness of strangers.
— A Streetcar Named Desire, 1951
Elia Kazan, dir.

4. NUTS AND BOLTS

Okay, are you ready to begin *actually* producing? Well, I'll let you in on a little secret...you've actually been producing already.

Now that you've got your brand, your list of assets, you've decided what type of project you want to do and you've begun writing it (or you've asked a friend to do so)—what's next? Now is when the rubber meets the road, so to speak. Now we talk about guerilla filmmaking vs. professional filmmaking. And no, these aren't necessarily professional terms—these are just *my* terms for what people do, everyday.

Guerilla Filmmaking

This is what some people call "run-and-gun," and it's basically this: you get a camera, a couple of friends who are actors, you go to the park, or your apartment or wherever, and you shoot a scene. No permits, no insurance, nada. Maybe not even craft services—just a pizza or some burgers when you're finished (and maybe not even). This is filmmaking at its most primitive and, really, its most scary. Why? Because this is when that guy Murphy (you know the one—the one they made up the law about?) starts lurking around, making trouble. Murphy's Law states that whatever *can* go wrong *will* go wrong.

You see, since you're the Producer—you're the one in charge. That means that everyone reports to you, looks to you and, basically, you're responsible for everyone on the set—the cast and the crew. If all goes well, then give yourself a pat on the back and breathe a sigh of relief. But if someone gets hurt—say trips over a rock, a piece of the set or just accidentally (you know, goofing around) falls, breaks an arm or a leg? Well, you're responsible. Which means you need to pay for their visit to urgent care (or the hospital if it's more serious than that). If that person happens to be an actor who makes their living as a waiter, and they broke their arm, you are required to pay their lost wages for those six weeks (or longer) while they recover. That is, unless you got Workman's Comp insurance. You did get that, right? Oh, hmm. Did you know that it's against the law in California to not have Workman's Comp insurance and you could get hit with a big fat fine for not carrying Workman's Comp? I know, I know — you're just doing a little New Media project, they're all your friends and no one is going to say anything. But are you sure? What if they get hurt, they can't work and they really need the money? Look, if you're like me you've never been hurt on a film set and that's great. But that's not to say it will never happen. And it's the last thing you *want* to have happen to someone on YOUR film set. Better safe than sorry I always say.

Next, let's talk about that camera that you rented; and those lights. None of the rental houses in town (at least in L.A. and probably elsewhere, too) will rent to you without proof of insurance. So, you're going to need to get insurance to rent that stuff. Maybe you can borrow a camera and some lights from your friend who went to film school. Yay, you! Then you don't actually need insurance, right? Wrong. Something could still go wrong. Someone could damage that camera or you could drop that camera. Your friend won't just say "Hey, no problem. I'll pay to get it fixed," or "I'll pay to get a new one." Uh, no, dude. He'll want you to pay to get it fixed or buy him a new one. Can you afford to do that? Getting insurance is less expensive than buying a new camera.

Oh, and your friend's parents, the ones who are letting you use their home for one of the locations? They're going to want you to have insurance protecting them from any liability should someone slip and fall on their property. They don't want one of your actor friends suing them if they slip and fall.

If you're using that bar that you work at during their off hours—you know the one—well, the owner of the place will require you to give him evidence of liability insurance, just in case one of your actors or crew hurts himself in his bar. He doesn't want to be hit with any claims either.

And finally, let's talk about permits. Most cities and counties in the U.S. will allow you to shoot in their municipality if you clear it with them first. Why? Because they want to know that someone is filming something, for any number of reasons. The main reason is that they, too, have liability that they want covered. This usually involves getting a permit to shoot at whatever location you want to use. Some of these permits are free. Some of them cost you money. Shooting without a permit, guerilla style, only seems attractive because it would, in some cases, save you money. But bear in mind that, especially in Los Angeles County, if you are found to be shooting without a permit you *will* be shut down. Immediately. No begging, no questions asked. Just shut down. That's a day lost. All your planning, actors and money spent to organize that day down the drain. Do people shoot in L.A. without permits? Yes, every day. Do I think it's a wise idea? No. Can you shoot in your own home/apartment/backyard without a permit? Yes. Legally? No. People are always flabbergasted when I tell them that. "Wh...wh...why?!" they ask. "It's my house/apartment/property." Yes, it is. But the City wouldn't let you open a restaurant there and sell food without a permit—and yet you have a kitchen. You can't shoot a movie/web series there without a permit.

True story: I was shadowing a director on a feature and we had a big day planned to shoot at the DP's (Director of Photography) house - in his garage. Bright and early in the morning the cast and crew arrived and began setting everything up and about an hour later the set was all lit and ready to go (around 8am). Just before the Director called 'Action' there was a knock at the door. It was the Fire

Marshall wanting to see the permit. It was at that point that the Producer did a disappearing act and the Director had to handle everything (not the last time this would happen on this shoot, unfortunately). So, no permit meant we were shut down. Done for the day. Um, no. We were on a 16-day schedule and couldn't *afford* to lose an entire day. So, the Director sent the cast and crew to the nearest mini-mall and he and I reconnoitered with the script to figure out how we would salvage the rest of the day which, thankfully, we did. But can you see how even trying to shoot at *your own house* can end up being a problem if one of your neighbors decides they don't like the extra people or cars in the neighborhood?

Professional Filmmaking

This is where you dot the i's and cross the t's. At it's most basic it means you get your insurance and you have permits. At it's more complex, it's where all the actors and crew are paid (which means that you've likely hired a payroll company) you're fully insured, you have all your permits and you're running a professional set, with craft services, catering (not pizzas)... in other words—a well-oiled machine. It may cost a little bit more, but the headaches you avoid *and* the peace of mind you have by being professional is worth the extra money, in my opinion.

I have given you my own opinion on the nuts and bolts of producing, meaning guerilla vs. professional. Please be aware that I am not telling you that you have to do it one way or the other. Also be aware that, even as there are two ends of the spectrum, there are a host of positions in between those two ends. There is no right or wrong way to do things—I am just telling you what I am comfortable with. I want you to have all the facts before you go out into the world to produce anything so that you don't get caught by surprise.

Oh, and be aware that different municipalities, even within the Southern California area, have different rules and pricing structures with regard to permits. Film LA[vi] covers Los Angeles County. But it doesn't cover Valencia, Santa Monica, Burbank, Orange County, Long Beach, any of the beaches — in fact lots of places around Southern California. Those all have their own permitting organizations with their own rules. So, it pays to check out *exactly* where you're going to be filming as each area's rules are different and some are more lenient (and less expensive) than others. This is another one of those areas where you might find that setting a scene in a slightly different locale saves you a boatload of money due to the cost of permits from one city to another.

You may be pleasantly surprised to find that in the area where you want to film, if the property is privately owned and the owner has given you their permission, you won't even *need* a permit. On the other hand, you may find out that the requirements are *so strict* that you decide not to film in that particular area AT ALL. Both of these things happened recently on films I produced. It doesn't help to tell you exactly where they were, since the permitting offices change their requirements randomly, without advance warning, and I don't want to mislead you by listing the areas here only to have them be different when you go there yourself. My advice to you is to do your research to find the best, most cost-effective locations for your production.

People are afraid of what they don't understand.
—Man of Steel, 2013
Zack Snyder, dir.

5: Yikes!! Producing Isn't Free

Okay, so the first thing you're going to learn is that producing isn't free. Nope. Sorry. It costs money to produce anything. Now, there are some ways to get around that and we've already discussed some of them here.

First, if you made your list of assets, then you're already ahead of the game. Why? Because each asset on that list represents something that you'll be able to get (i.e., put into your production) for little to no money. If it belongs to you, then YAY! You've got it for free. If it belongs to a good friend who supports you in your career, you can probably get it for free as well. If it belongs to a colleague or associate, someone you don't know quite as well, then you may need to barter for it. But notice I said "barter." Start thinking about what you do well that you can exchange with people. Say you are particularly good at making websites in WordPress. Offer to do your friend's website in exchange. Say your friend is also an actor – offer to run lines with her the next time she has an audition or is doing a self-tape. I'm sure you can get creative with the things that you can offer up.

There *will* be some things for which you will have to pay. There's just no getting around that. So, how do you do that? I can't necessarily answer that question for you, but I can give you some suggestions:

First, perhaps you'll consider this project an investment in your career. When I made my first short film I had not attended film school, nor did I intend to. Nope. I had been a working actress for a number of years and considered my time on set, study of films and shadowing other filmmakers to *be* my film school. I was making that film not only to showcase my skills as an actor and put my own brand out there in a big way, but also to showcase myself as a writer/director and producer. So, I had no qualms about investing my own money into the project—it was less than tuition at film school, and certainly less than tuition at film school *plus* the amount I would've had to pay to produce my film school project(s).

Perhaps you were thinking about approaching one of those "tape scenes for your demo reel" type of places, but decided you wanted to have a little more control over the project and do it yourself. When you actually price out what those places cost, you might find that doing it yourself and investing the money into your own project isn't all that different from paying someone else. The end product you get when you do it yourself may be more to your liking.

Another way to go about financing the project is to decide on the venue—short film, web series, etc—put together your cast, and then you and your cast-mates go in together on the financing of the piece. If the project is an ensemble web series where everyone's part is written to showcase their brand and each actor is also a producer, that isn't an unreasonable request. Particularly when you've been able to reduce the costs by putting together a bunch of assets before even beginning the process. Make sure you put together a written agreement, spelling out what each person's contribution to the project is and what each person will receive from the project, so that there aren't any misunderstandings later on down the road. This can be a nifty way to finance an inexpensive web series. Especially if you can keep costs to a minimum by reducing shooting days, locations and other expenses.

There are some crowd-funding sources you can investigate, including Indiegogo[vii] and Kickstarter[viii], where you put up a pitch for your project and people donate money to it. It's based on the concept that if everyone puts in a little bit, then you'll have a lot. These work particularly well if (a) you have a big following or fan group, and (b) you are willing to spend as much time promoting your campaign as you are going to on your project. They don't work particularly well if you just put up a campaign, hit "start," and hope it works all on its own. Again, that old adage of "you get out of it what you put into it" comes into play here.

I have friends who have been creative about financing their projects: some have mounted fund-raising activities like a themed party with door prizes where the donation at the door and the raffle tickets were part of the fund-raising effort; others have had garage sales and emptied out their closets, garages and friends' closets and garages, and sold stuff in order to raise money. There are many creative ways you can go about raising money. In fact, I want YOU to be creative and think of something unusual and fun, and then let me know how you did it. Tweet me with your very own interesting, fun way you raised money for your project.

There have also been those who decided to finance their projects, even feature films, on credit cards. I wouldn't recommend doing that. First, for the types of projects you're likely to do—shorts and new media—the financial return is minimal, at best. There are a *few* outlets where these things can be sold and make some money (and we'll cover those in Distribution), but there's no guarantee that they will make back their budget and go into profits. So, you'd be better off saving your money. If you want or need to go the route of borrowing money to get your project made, I think the best way to go about it is to go to a close friend or wealthy family member who supports your career and offer to pay them back over time—with a lower interest rate or *no* interest at all, if you can swing it.

Finally—and here you can get really creative—are there things about your project or your script that would appeal to another brand in the marketplace? What am I talking about? Well, let me explain. When I put together my first short film, *Reflections of a Life*, it was a film about a woman who confronts a diagnosis of breast cancer. I knew that there were many organizations out there that have breast cancer as a cause. So, I contacted one of them—a woman's clothing store—and asked if they would donate the wardrobe for the female characters in the film. They did! It was pretty awesome! I also found a man who had written a book, *Cancer for Two*, and asked him if he would send me the book. He did. I read it, loved it and asked him if I could use one line from it *in the movie*. He agreed. In exchange I put the book on the counter in one of the scenes of the movie, as though the character was reading it. That author later went on tour with me, to several film festivals, and signed books as part of the promotion that we did on the festival circuit. We are still close friends today. I've heard about people approaching local bakeries for bagels (for craft services), local coffee shops to supply a steady stream of coffee for filming, T-shirts, ball-caps (if you can get the entire crew to wear a logo T-shirt and/or ballcap don't you think someone would want to supply that *and* maybe donate some money to the cause?). There are just so many ways to go about doing this, I'm sure you'll be able to think of a very creative way for your project.

My only caution is this: if you're producing your project under a SAG/AFTRA contract you'll want to check to be sure that you don't fall under what they call their "commercials" clause or contract by accepting cash in exchange for putting products or product placement in your short or web series. The last time I was putting together a web series that was looking to raise money and inquired about an exchange of cash for product placement, the SAG/AFTRA representative told me that if we took the cash it would put us under the commercials contract, which would mean that every time the web series showed anywhere I (as the producer) would be responsible for paying the actors residuals. Um, no. Couldn't afford to do that. Sorry. I love actors (I am one) and I usually try to pay them in every project I do, but when you're doing one of these shoestring budget projects you can't afford to pay residuals just because the project is on the internet. Nevertheless, the contracts may have changed since then so be sure to check it out for yourself.

However you raise the money for your project, you'll be glad you put your list of assets in place first, which will help you save, save, save.

Show me the money!
—Jerry Maguire, 1996
Cameron Crowe, dir.

Part Two: Pre-Production

If you build it, he will come
　—Field of Dreams, 1989
　Phil Alden Robinson, dir.

6: Your Team

Besides the actors that you have in your project, you're going to want to have crew members. On a film set these people are considered "below-the-line". The "above-the-line" personnel are considered the actors, the producers, the writer and the director. The below-the-line personnel are everyone else. These include: production design (art department, props, set design), DP (Director of Photography) or cinematographer and his department (camera assistants, gaffer, grips), Assistant Director (AD and 2nd AD), Script Supervisor (Scripty), Unit Production Manager and Line Producer and the PAs, makeup and hair, wardrobe or costume design and choreography (if you have dancing in your project) or stunts (if you have fighting or car chases) in your project.

You don't necessarily need to have an individual to fill each one of these positions, but each one of these positions must be 'handled,' meaning someone must do the job of each one of these positions. For instance, one person could handle makeup *and* hair, and one person could be the Unit Production Manager *and* the Line Producer, as well as being one of the above-the-line producers on the project. It all depends on how big your project is and what the budget allows. Each one of these jobs needs to be done so that your project flows smoothly, what you want and need to end up on the screen actually gets there *and* so that you stay on time and on budget (see the Appendix for a more detailed description of each job, when they are hired and how to hire someone qualified for the job). There's nothing worse than a disorganized set where people are running around not knowing who is doing what, what needs to be done next, and you don't "make your day," meaning you don't shoot the pages (scenes) that need to get shot that day. When that happens you either need to (a) come back to that location the next day (or a future day) with all your cast, crew and equipment, and shoot the scenes you couldn't get done when you wanted to or (b) scrap those scenes altogether. Neither one of these choices is ideal.

Here's where I'll stress pre-planning. The more time you spend in pre-production the smoother your production should flow. Time spent in pre-production includes gathering and obtaining all the props you'll need; speaking with each of your department heads to let them know exactly what you need from them so they can plan what they need to do to be prepared; working with your First AD to plan the shoot so that each day has a doable number of scenes/shots with the right combination of actors and doesn't force your production to move around from location to location; letting all your location owners know, in advance, when you'll be wanting/needing to shoot at their space and clearing it with them so that it will be smooth sailing on the day of production; and clearing the schedules of your actors.

One of the things I recommend doing early is to work on obtaining your insurance. This is one of those things that takes time and you don't want to end up down to the wire with no insurance, which could mean no shoot. Even if you don't have all the information necessary to finalize the quote, starting the process early will mean that you'll have your insurance when you need it. You can always adjust the dates of your shoot with your carrier — if your shoot gets pushed — so that the insurance coverage starts when your shoot starts. As long as you're working with an agent that shouldn't be a problem. However, I suggest that you don't actually make the *payment* for the insurance until everything (locations, dates, etc.) is locked in.

One of the things I recommend doing last — near the start of production — is obtaining your permit(s). This is because you want to be sure that none of your locations 'fall out' at the last minute, forcing you to either (a) find a new location; (b) adjust your script to shoot those scenes at one of your other locations, adding a day (or more) to that location (which may take some finagling and permission from them); or (c) scrapping the shooting schedule altogether while you search for a new location and then regroup and reschedule everything to start again. If you've bought your permits you can't go back or get a refund, which means more money spent on permits when you *finally* put the shoot back on track.

On my first short film, *Reflections of a Life*, we had that exact situation happen: a beautiful wedding scene was going to be shot at a friend's house—a wonderful location in the hills, with beautiful tall trees and grass...just a lovely setting. At the very, very last minute (after I had clicked "submit" online to obtain the appropriate permit) she got cold feet, deciding that maybe it wasn't going to be a good idea to have a dozen actors in and out of the house, using the bathroom (to change, etc.) and where *were* we going to put our craft services anyway? Aaarrgghh! So, we found another location, which ended up being better than the first, but since I had already submitted my online application we were forced to pay the minimum amount for the permit which, even then, was pretty substantial. Lesson learned.

Choosing Your Team

It has been noted that in Hollywood people often work with some of the same cast and crew over and over again. This is true. I believe that once you start working in this business, you establish working relationships with various cast and crew members and, if you like working with them, you continue to work together—forming a team—thereby minimizing risk. I highly recommend it.

You should strive to find people—good people—for your projects and treat them well so that they want to work with you again. Then bring them back to work with you on your next project. This is what I've done.

How do you do this? When you embark on your first

project it helps if you have a clear vision of what you want to accomplish: what you want that project to communicate, how you want it to look and what the feel of it should be so that you can convey that clearly to each department (hmm, knowing the 'why' back from Chapter 2 seems like the answer here). Then you interview people. You put out the word. The best way to start is through your networks. Bonnie Gillespie refers to this as going through your "web of trust." These are the people you have worked with before and, therefore, you trust. See who they know and who they have worked with and who they recommend. Understand that in this business a recommendation is hard to come by. Why? Because people stake their reputations on their recommendations. If I give you a bad recommendation you will think less of *me*. But if I give you a good recommendation—someone who works well with you and contributes to your project—you'll be singing MY praises right along with the person I recommended. See how that works?

For starters, you'll want to meet and talk with these people. See if you click. Find out what they've done. Look at their IMDb[ix], look at their reel and find out if the way they work matches the way you want to work. Ask about their vision of the project and see if it matches yours. It's a process, for sure, but one that will yield relationships that will last you the rest of your life, both in and out of the business.

Certainly, if you're a working actor you'll find yourself on many different sets working with many different production personnel—even student films and indie films. Talk to them. Get to know them. Form relationships with these people. Don't just go and sit in your trailer, or holding area, while you're waiting to be called. Sit on the sidelines and carefully watch how the different members of the crew work together. Then, when they're on a break or not too busy, ask them about their job. People in this business usually love what they do and love to talk about it to a willing listener. BE that willing listener. You may just find that you establish some relationships with people who will want to work with you. This is how I've found some of my key team members over the years.

I have been building my team since before I started on my first project, *Reflections of a Life*, in 2005. There are people who worked on that project that have worked on every project with me since. Same with *Worth*. I added a few more people on that project—people who have been with me since that project. With each project there have also been people that didn't stick—people who came in for just that one project and weren't brought back. I think that's the way it goes with each project. You add a few people, some of whom stick and some of whom just come in for that particular project and fade away, never to work with you again. Some of the people who have been with me for many of my projects I found when I was working as an actress on someone else's project. I liked their style. When it came time for me to put my own project together, I contacted them and asked them to work with me.

Don't feel bad about those who come in just for one project and fade away. They contributed to that project and you added to their resume. Unfortunately, they just didn't make the cut to end up on the team. Or their availability changed. It happens. Perhaps you'll work with them again sometime in the future.

And one thing I'll caution you—people DO change. I've had people who were absolutely fabulous for one project who, by the time we came together on the next project, had completely changed and our styles no longer meshed. It happens. Let it go and let them go. No hard feelings. If you find that someone's energy or demeanor is bringing a project down, you gotta let them go before it brings the whole project down. Don't hold onto someone out of misplaced loyalty. Yes, give them the benefit of the doubt. But when they've made their position absolutely clear, and it doesn't jive with yours, then it's time to let go.

Let's talk a little bit about paying people...yes, I'm going to bring that up. I understand that when you're embarking on your first couple of projects you may not have a lot of money to spend (you don't have a rich grandfather? LOL!). So, you can't pay people and you want them to work for free, or what we refer to in the business as "copy, credit, meals." Lots of people understand that, particularly if they're at your tier (level) or just above. They know that it's difficult to fund a project when you're first starting because, hey, you're just starting! Does that mean you can't get good people for your project? No! You can get excellent people for your project. You will just have to understand, though, that you aren't going to be able to attract people at a much higher tier. Those people get paid—this is what they do for a living and they generally can't afford to do it for free. If you find someone who has a little free time and wants to come play with you, that's awesome! Lucky you. Otherwise, you'll want to find the best, most talented people at *your* tier—or just above—who believe in you and your project and want to get involved. What you'll find is that you all tend to rise up together—meaning you all tend to rise to the next tier at about the same time and you'll just continue to work together year after year.

Here's the thing, though: treat these people well, feed them well, *give* them their copy and credit (and, of course, those good meals) and when you move up to the next tier, take them with you. I know that just makes good sense, but you can't imagine how many times people I know in various crafts (DPs, editors, etc.) have been wooed into a project with the promise, "I know we don't have any money for *this* project, but this is going to lead to much better things and when those happen you'll be our first choice..." and they went ahead and did the project for little to no money. *Then* when the projects with money came along, the producers hired someone else! Let me repeat that. When the project with money came along—THE PRODUCER HIRED SOMEONE

ELSE. Really?? What a douche move. Don't do that. If the people worked for you, did a good job for you and were generally positive to be around—reward them by hiring them on the next project when there is money. Don't just figure "Now I have money I can get so-and-so (insert 'bigger name' actor/crew member here)."

Now, of course, when you're looking to hire actors on that bigger budget project, you may *need* a name to sell your project to distributors, but look out for a nice, juicy, smaller part for that friend who helped you on your freebie. This is how you reward them for helping you get to the place where you even have that opportunity to cast a name in a project. Of course, the same goes for the various crew positions—if the producer has someone specific that *they* want to hire for the project, try to find a position for that crew member who helped on your lower-budget projects. Or bring them into the next project where you have a little more say-so.

Now you've got your perfect script. It's full of your assets and tailored to you. You've lined up your personnel, your insurance and permits—if you're shooting professionally. Let's move onward towards production.

7: Union, Permits, Insurance

You're finally getting ready for production. Your script is written; you've lined up your actors and your location(s); your crew is coming together; you've got a budget and some money. What else is there? You should just be able to go shoot, right? Well…almost. There are still a few decisions that need to be made.

Union or Not?

One of the first things you'll want to decide is: union or no? Obviously, if you're a SAG/AFTRA member you'll want to do this under a union contract. If you're not, then you have a couple of options. You can do it under a Union contract and possibly (note I said *possibly* here) Taft-Hartley yourself, or you can skip the unions altogether. Even if you do it under a union contract and you're not a union member, there are still union contracts under which you *can* hire yourself, without doing the Taft/Hartley paperwork (if you'd prefer to stay non-Union).

Since the unions merged a few years ago and the contracts have been rewritten a couple times since then, I'm not going to go into a long explanation of how all the different contracts work. They *may* change by the time you read this. What I *will* say is that at the moment I write this, the lower *film* contracts, meaning the SAG/AFTRA ultra-low budget indie, short film, short form and student film contract all allow for union members to work with non-union members in the same project—all working side-by-side in speaking parts. *However*, these contracts DO NOT allow for Taft-Hartleying the non-union actors into the union. The first contract that *does* allow for Taft-Hartley (as far as film contracts go) is the modified-

low. However, the *New Media* contract *currently* allows for Taft-Hartley, as long as at least one member of the cast is a union member (again, check with the SAG/AFTRA website or check with your rep as these can change by the time you read this book).

And what is Taft-Hartley, you ask? Again, there are places you can go to read all about this interesting bit of legislation[x]. Suffice it to say that it is a piece of legislation that says you can't close a union to new members and must allow a way for new members to join.

Anyway, your first decision is whether or not you'll do your project under a union contract and, if your decision is to do so, you need to file the appropriate paperwork. I would suggest, if you are going union, you start the process of filing that paperwork at least six to eight weeks in advance of when you plan to shoot as it can take that long to process and approve it. However, as far as SAG/AFTRA goes, there is a handy way to do this online[xi].

Also, SAG/AFTRA has cool indie workshops that explain, in detail, how all the current contracts work. Check to see if they're having one in your area and register to attend — they're free and you do not need to be a SAG/AFTRA member to attend since they're designed to give this information to actors who want to produce as well as producers who want to hire union actors.

Permits and Insurance

You'll want to start investigating all of these things as soon as you set a date — or sooner if possible — so that you can put the figures into your budget. As I said before, you don't want to actually pull the trigger on your permit until you've locked everything in — usually about a week to 10 days before production starts. However, knowing where you need to go, online, to file the paperwork for the permits, or which government entity you'll need to call and even calling and starting the process and getting a rep for both your permits and your insurance, is a timesaver.

You should also know that the insurance process can take even longer than the permit process. Start that as soon as you set a date for production, even if it's a tentative date and even if that is weeks before you'll actually be in production. This gives you time to price out the various options and select the best insurance for the best price.

Pray for the best, prepare for the worst.
—Prisoners, 2013
Denis Villenueve, dir.

8: Scheduling

If you've got a first or second (or second 2nd) AD (Assistant Director) for your production, they'll most likely want to meet with you and put together a shooting schedule based on the availability of the actors, locations and such. If *you're* acting as the AD—or your AD is inexperienced—then you'll want to know how to go about doing that scheduling yourself. As the producer it doesn't hurt to understand how scheduling is done. Oh, and if this is your first time producing anything and you're shooting for more than one day I just have one question for you – ARE YOU CRAZY??!! Really, if this is your first go-'round, you should be thinking in the simplest terms possible. Meaning a one-day shoot, one location with two or three actors. That's it. Anything more than that and you're taking on a LOT for a first-timer. But hey, if you're game and you want to know how to schedule for a more extensive shoot, read on.

It's simple really…and yet complex at the same time. You need to keep two principles in mind:

(1) Every time that the cast and crew move from one location to another is called a 'company move.' Every time you make a company move it's going to cost you several hours of time, which means money. You want to avoid unnecessary moves, which means shooting all the scenes that happen at the same location on the same day.

(2) Book your actors so that their scenes happen in succession and an actor's scenes are all grouped together on the same day or back-to-back days. If that actor is a 'name' or 'semi-name', and you're paying them under the SAG/AFTRA contract, you do not want to have a day in-between (where

they don't shoot). You might end up having to pay for that day in-between, depending on the contract under which you're shooting. I recommend you read the contract carefully (or make sure your AD knows the contracts well). Also, you have less risk of that actor booking another job and canceling on you—which they have the right to do under the lower contracts like the Short Film Agreement—particularly if they book something like a large feature or a pilot.

Having many characters in the story and several locations can make scheduling pretty complex. If that is the nature of your project, you'd be better off hiring an experienced AD or line producer to coordinate all the logistics. If you have a fairly simple story, with only a couple of different locations and a few actors, it shouldn't be too difficult to schedule all the scenes that take place in one location and film them on the same day. It does not matter if you shoot the scenes out of order.

If there is a second location, film *all* the scenes that happen at that second location on the second day. It is not efficient to begin filming at one location on the first day and then move to a second location on the same day. It takes time and money to break down the equipment, set it up at the next location, *and* move everyone from one location to another.

If you want to shoot a web series and you're trying to save money, I generally recommend that you set it all at one location—maybe two. My web series, *Mom & Me*, was set in the mom's house and filmed in the house of the actress. Her character was eclectic and a throwback to the '60s hippie lifestyle and the actress who played that character lived in a house that was absolutely perfect. No set dressing required. There were a couple of scenes where we left that one location (which were filmed on a different day), but we filmed all 12 episodes primarily in that one location over two days. Because we did that, we were able to film the bulk of the series in two days. Another web series, *A Cup of Confusion*, takes place in an office and goes back and forth between a conference room and a break room. Both locations were in the same space, so it was as if we were shooting in one location as well. These are the types of situations where you can shoot multiple episodes in a weekend (or two-day shoot), or if you've written a tight, economical script with just a few actors, just one day.

This is one of the reasons I recommend, especially for your first and second project, that you confine yourself to one location and a minimum of characters. Not only does it save you money (in terms of obtaining the locations and permits for those locations) but it will also save you time, since you can usually get your shooting done in just a day or two.

Bear in mind that if you're renting equipment many rental houses consider Saturday and Sunday to be *one* day. This means that you'll be paying for your camera and lights for one day but, since you'll be picking them up Friday afternoon and returning them Monday morning, you'll essentially have two full days and another half day (Friday night) in which to shoot your project—more bang for your buck! If it's an especially complex shoot, with a fancy camera (Arri Alexa, RED) having that extra half-day may come in useful as a 'set-up' day. It can allow you to set up your camera and lights at your location so that when you arrive the next morning you can hit the ground running and you're not spending the first couple of hours getting set up for filming, although you will still need to get your actors into makeup, hair and wardrobe. However, that ought to take less time than setting up your lights, camera and set. This can be especially helpful when you've only got one day.

Fasten your seatbelts. It's going to be a bumpy night.
— All About Eve, 1950
Joseph L. Mankiewicz

9: Script Breakdown

The next thing you want to do in pre-production is a breakdown of the script itself. If you wrote the script (or co-wrote it) you might be saying to yourself, "Hey, I wrote this thing, I don't need to break it down—I know it inside and out." Well, yes and no. You *think* you know it inside and out. When it comes to shooting a project, you don't really *know* it the way each department head needs to know it and the way *you* need to know it in order to communicate what you want to each department.

I recommend going through the script with different colored highlighter pens. This is how I do it:

Yellow = character
Green = Props
Blue = Wardrobe
Pink = Vehicles
Grey/Purple = Production Notes

I make a key at the top of the script or on the title page, using the highlighters as a visual reference. I go through the script, one time for each color/category. Again, you'll think you can do it all—or at least *two* categories—at the same time. Don't try. It will become overwhelming and you'll miss something.

I start on page one and as I read through, each time a character is referenced in the narrative portion (not the dialogue), I highlight their mention in yellow. I do this for the entire script.

Then I read through again. Each time a prop is specified, either in the narrative or in dialogue, I highlight that mention in green. Third time through, each time a specific piece of wardrobe is described, I highlight that in blue. Fourth time through, each time a vehicle is mentioned I highlight that in pink. And the final time, each time there are production notes or anything I want to stand out and remember, I highlight that in grey or purple –whichever color I can get.

Most of the highlighting will be done in the narrative – or action – portions of the script, although there are occasional highlights in the dialogue when reference is made to the handling of a prop or piece of wardrobe. Again, don't try to do it all in one pass.

Why do I do this? Well, as you'll begin to see when you do it the first time, it's going to 'highlight' things about your script that you probably weren't aware of. Like how many different props you actually need in order to accomplish shooting the script that you wrote – or had written for you; how specific the clothing is; which characters are needed for which scenes. It's an excellent way to see exactly how to organize your shoot in terms of scheduling and exactly what preparations you'll need to do in your pre-production period.

Character

We've talked about how to schedule your actors so that they do all their scenes on the same day or, if they work multiple days, they do them back-to-back. By highlighting the characters, you'll be able to actually *see* how this works – you'll be able to see which characters populate which scenes.

Now you need to make another list. Start with Day 1. Where are you shooting on Day 1 – what location? Which *other* scenes take place at that location? Go to those scenes in your highlighted script. If you're going to shoot all of those scenes on Day 1 (and you should) you'll need to know everything required for that day – especially which actors you'll need for every scene. See how easy this is? Continue the same thing for Day 2 and so on.

Props

Now go back to Day 1. Go back through your script and make a list of the props you will need for that day. They will be highlighted in your script in green. You will know which ones you need because you already know which scenes you're shooting on Day 1. Add these props to your list for Day 1. Do this for every day you're shooting. If you have a Production Designer, an Art Department Supervisor or Set Decorator they will do this as well, but it's nice to know what's needed so you can backstop them. Often, on low-budget shoots, *you* are the Production Designer or Set Decorator and going to be responsible for not only obtaining the props but for making sure they are brought to the set on the right day. So doing this breakdown will be invaluable to you.

Wardrobe

Do the same thing for specific wardrobe for each day. If you have a wardrobe person, they will also do this but again, as the producer, you should know what is needed for each day. This way you can be sure that the wardrobe person not only has the proper wardrobe prepared in advance of the shoot, but comes prepared to each day's location. Be aware that on low-budget shoots the actors often wear their own clothes. This is fine, but if you are shooting scenes out of order you'll want to make sure that *someone* makes a note of what the actors are wearing in every scene for continuity purposes. You don't want your actor wearing a black T-shirt in one shot in the kitchen and suddenly, as he steps into the backyard (as a continuation of the same scene), he's now wearing a blue button-down, collared shirt. That would be very jarring indeed.

Vehicles

Very often you won't have a property master or

someone who will be responsible for vehicles in a low budget project. That person will be you. So this is particularly important. Often in low budget projects you won't even have vehicles in the project. But if you do, you had better stay on top of it and make sure that you know what vehicles will be needed for which day. You don't want your hero driving a BMW away from his apartment in one scene and arriving in a Chevy in the next scene because the person with the BMW wasn't notified that the car was needed on the second day. Trust me, I've seen it happen. Or, I've seen the workaround when the first car isn't available on the second day and the director has to decide to scrap the scene of the hero arriving and film him already there.

Production Notes

These are random production notes—but they are anything but random. This is, basically, where you put everything else. Anything that doesn't fit in any of the above categories. Stuff like "a dark shadow passes over her face" or "jump into the pool" or "track through the crowd." These are the types of things you want to keep track of for each day so that you know what the writer wanted in that scene. Now, a good director is going to make sure that these things are well taken care of. But that doesn't mean that you shouldn't make a note of them yourself. A good producer will also come prepared to make sure that these specific production notes are handled in the days' shoot as well.

Let's take the "jump into the pool" note, for instance. When you go to shoot that scene, you *do* know that after each take the actor (or actress) will have to towel off, have their hair and makeup completely re-done and have a dry set of clothing waiting for them so that they can start the next take dry, right? So, in order to make sure that you maximize your day, you'll want to shoot this part of the scene last (and hope your actors and director get it in the first take).

Same thing with any scene involving squibs (blood effects) and/or special makeup fx. These scenes will involve extra time for the makeup department (or person if there isn't a whole department) and you'll need to take care that clean-up happens between takes so that the residual blood and other mess isn't visible at the beginning of the scene. Oh, and if you're shooting with blood fx you'll want to protect the surrounding set pieces (unless you're shooting outside) so that you won't incur a hefty cleaning bill.

One final note: the kissing scenes. I think producers (and directors) often forget that the actors' makeup often gets completely 'undone' in a kissing scene—lipstick gets transferred from the woman to the man and there can be a bit of 'razor burn' type sensitivity rash that can form on a woman's face in a particularly passionate scene. These types of things would require a complete re-do of the makeup for both parties so that's something to keep in mind.

Having these notes highlighted in advance allows you to pre-plan how and when you will shoot these scenes for maximum savings of time and money.

A good plan today is better than a perfect plan tomorrow.
— Wag the Dog, 1997
Barry Levinson, dir

Part Three: Production

Carpe diem. Seize the day, boys.
Make your lives extraordinary.
— Dead Poets Society, 1989
Peter Weir, dir

10: Final Checklist

Okay, you're ready to go, right? Well...almost. You just need to go through a little checklist to make sure you've done all your pre-planning. As you can see by now, planning and preparation are the keys to a successful shoot. Hopefully you've spent so much time in those preparatory stages that the production will breeze by and be so much fun you'll wonder where it all went.

So let's look at all your pre-production stages and see if there's any last-minute items you still need to check off your list: Make sure:

1. You've scheduled your actors, your crew and your locations and everyone knows where to be when.

2. The equipment is all lined up and someone is designated to pick up and check out the equipment and make sure it's ready to go.

3. You have plenty of blank media (whatever you're going to use to record onto).

4. You have batteries that are all charged.

5. All your props are in one place and someone is responsible for getting them to the location(s) and keeping track of them.

6. You have someone providing food for your cast and crew (a VERY necessary item—especially if you're asking people to work on the cheap).

7. Your SAG/AFTRA paperwork is filed and approved (if you're shooting union).

8. Your insurance is bought and approved, along with your permits (if you're shooting professionally, of course ;-)).

9. Your key crew members all know who's responsible for what before, during and after the shoot.

STOP. Don't go any further. If you haven't got contracts and releases signed or ready to be signed for all the cast and crew you need to do that immediately. You should never go into production, expose one frame of film, utter the word "Action," pass "Go," collect $200... okay, you get the idea, right? It doesn't matter if this is a big production or the teeny, tiniest little 'let's get together and shoot a little something in my living room' kind of project, you should get everything, and I mean EVERYTHING spelled out in writing and signed and dated before you actually go into production. Why?

Oh well, can I tell you the horror stories of people who were going into production with their friends on a small project (web series, short film, it doesn't really matter does it?) and only after it was all done someone changed their mind about the storyline, the way it should be edited... something, and took the raw footage and changed it all to suit their vision of the project? These sorts of things happen. You don't want it to happen to you.

Oh, and you did get something in writing with your writer if someone else wrote your project, didn't you? Because the last thing you want is to have a problem with the writer who then comes and repossesses the footage *after* you've spent all sorts of money to hire actors and crew and shoot it because you didn't stick with the way they saw the script.

Horror stories? Yes. Don't let it happen to you.

Okay, back to our original final checklist:

It would be a good idea to have a final production meeting a day or two before the start of production with your key crew (director, 1st, DP, wardrobe, production designer and stunt coordinator, if there is one). This is where you'll discover any last-minute situations or problems that need to be addressed. You'll also be able to go over any concerns.

If you have a First (or second) AD their job will be to confirm with the actors the night before they are needed and to send out the Call Sheets. The Call Sheets are those sheets of paper (emailed these days) that have all the information about the next day's shoot on them: where the location is, where the parking is, what the call time is for the crew and each member of the cast (when they report to makeup and when they report to set), what scenes will be shot on that particular day, any notes regarding specific items of wardrobe or props that will be needed so that those crew members can remember to bring those items, whether the shoot is indoors or outdoors and what the weather will be like, the location of the nearest hospital (yes, you might need this information in an emergency), and the phone number of the First AD and anybody else who may need to be reached late at night or early in the morning.

A 'Preliminary Call Sheet' is usually sent out (emailed) to cast and crew well in advance of the shoot (meaning at least a few days in advance) so people can block out their schedules and prepare for the shoot. This is also so that actors can prepare for when specific scenes need to be ready, stunt people can prepare for when stunt work will be happening and everyone can prepare for when a particularly troublesome scene (like an action scene with lots of set-ups) might be filming. So, once you're a few days (or a week) out from the start of production you will want to have your AD put together a Preliminary Call Sheet for production and send it out. A Final Call Sheet is sent out the night before for the next day's shoot, noting any changes in a different color (like Red).

First Day of Production

And now TA-DA!! The First Day of Production!! And what does a good producer do? You show up. You're there early. You stay late. You should be the first one on set and the last one to leave. What is your job? Well, if things are running smoothly it may be difficult to determine what your job actually is, because things are...running smoothly. Yay you!! You did a great job in pre-production and now you get to sit back, relax and watch the project shoot. Or, if you're in it (as a good self-producer you put yourself in a part, right?) you get to actually... act. YAY! But be aware that your job as producer has not really ended.

The producer's job during production is to roll with the punches—to be a problem-solver. To the extent that you can do that quickly, easily, without a lot of stress and without letting too many in the cast and crew know there's a problem determines how good a producer you actually are. For instance: it's the first day of production and you have a PA who didn't show up. What do you do? You reach out to your web of trust and get someone else to take his/her place. Your BMW fell out for the next day and you need a nice, luxury car. What do you do? You get on the phone and find something to take its place. There's a disagreement with the guy who's renting you the lighting and grip equipment. You get on the phone and work it out. You do all this without getting stressed, without letting the rest of the cast and crew know that there's a problem and without letting your performance (as an actor) suffer. Wow! Big job! Yes. Yes it is.

As it turns out, it seems that no matter how much time, effort and energy you put into pre-production there will always be *something* during production that has to be handled, fixed or re-done. However, don't let that lead you to believe that you should just leave everything till production to be handled. Yikes!!! That would be a nightmare of supreme proportions. Do your best in pre-pro so that you minimize the things that *could* go wrong during production and you will thank me.

This is one of those times that I tell people: you will learn more from actually *doing* this than you will from reading the book, hearing me speak or booking a coaching session.

Can I impart some of my wisdom to you? Of course. But you have to actually go through the process to understand all the different things that could possibly go wrong during production so that the next time around you prepare well enough to make sure that those things don't happen. But, then *other things* happen during that production that you never anticipated. So, on the project after that you add those to the list of 'things that have to be planned and prepared for,' in advance, so you will be sure that nothing will go awry during the next production and, sure enough, *something new* happens that you have to handle. And so it goes.

On each new project you will have something happen that you *never thought of before*. In fact, I'm not sure there is ever a production that goes completely smoothly, with no 'bumps in the road'. It's why people often say that they wonder how anything ever gets made in Hollywood. However, what *does* happen is that *you* get better and better at managing whatever comes up. That becomes your super power—your ability to handle *whatever* comes up.

And then, before you know it, and WAY before you're ready, the production is over and it's time to begin the post-production process.

Part Four: Post-Production

*Mama always said life was like a box of chocolates.
You never know what you're gonna get.*

—Forrest Gump, 1994
Robert Zemeckis, dir

11: On the Cutting Room Floor

Many, many people say that the film (web series, TV show, whatever) is really made in post and I believe it's true. Yes, you need a good script to begin with. It all starts with a good script. You can't do better than the original source material. And yes, you have to produce it well, execute that material to the best of your ability, with a good director, good actors and a good crew all working in harmony to make an awesome project.

But post-production is where the project really becomes a film, a TV show or a web series. This is where the magic happens. Learn to love this process and you will learn the secret of being a great producer.

Many producers abdicate the entire post-production process to their director, the editor or—if they have a little more money than that—a post-production supervisor. I think that's a big mistake. Yes, your director is going to play a big role in the post process. This is her baby and she'll want to shepherd it through and make sure that her vision remains intact throughout the process. Your post-production supervisor can be a BIG help to you as they (and you) negotiate with the various different pieces, people and vendors involved in this process, as well. But you should also be involved. This is your film/TV show/web series. Don't let someone else take the reigns at this point. At least stay involved enough to learn what post is all about.

Oh, and you did save some money for post, didn't you? This is the biggest mistake I see inexperienced producers make—they spend *all* their money in production and then they get to post and have nothing left. Yet this is where you're going to spend the most time and want the most expertise in order to really make your project a winner. Don't shortchange yourself and leave yourself nothing at this stage—and then decide that *you* can edit, write the music, mix and do everything else that it will take to get your film out the door or worse—try to get these all-important services for free. PLEASE!!

Here, let me teach you a little about the process so you can appreciate the craft and expertise that goes into this very important part of the filmmaking process.

Editing

The first thing that will happen on the project is that an editor will put together a rough cut. Now, this doesn't *just* happen. This can take hours and hours (and days and weeks) of time doing the following:

1. Ingesting the footage. This is where the footage is entered into the computer from the camera media so that the editor can manipulate it and put it together.

2. Transcoding the footage to work with the editor's editing software of choice. This step *might* be bypassed if the editor's software already recognizes the footage as it was shot. (This depends on what camera you used to shoot the footage and what editing software is being used to edit the footage.) If not, this step can take hours, days or even weeks, depending upon how much footage you shot and the size. Did you shoot 4K? 8K? (Don't scoff – it's coming!)

3. Syncing up the dailies. This is where the editor takes the picture and marries it with the sound track, putting them in sync. (You did record sound professionally, right? You didn't just use the mic on the camera. That would be a BIG faux pas.)

4. Now the editor is ready to assemble a rough cut.

You see all the work that has to happen *before* the scenes are cut together? That seems like a lot of busywork, but unless you have a lot of money for post, you won't be able to afford an assistant editor so your editor will be doing all that work him- or herself. This is the groundwork for doing the *actual* edit. Hopefully by now you're beginning to see the necessity for some money at this stage of the project. On bigger budget projects the assistants do all of this prep work. On your smaller-budget projects your editor will be doing all that prep work. Appreciate him or her. That's the thankless work — the stuff that's not fun.

I'm going to stress here — don't try to edit this yourself. Casting Director and producer Bonnie Gillespie calls this "The Island Syndrome." It's where the producer also takes on the jobs of lead actor, writer, director, craft services, composer, editor…you get the picture. There are very few people who can successfully do more than, say, 2 jobs on a project without the project starting to become too narrow in its vision. I think if you wrote the piece (or co-wrote it), produce it and act in it that's enough. Get some outside vision for your project — get some other people to share in its creation. This is a collaborative medium and projects are best created together as a collaboration of several creative minds.

Okay, back to editing. Once your editor has a rough cut, they'll want you to see it. Now, you may have been sitting in on the editing throughout the process and have already seen the rough cut. However, at this point you and the director (and anyone else you'd like to bring in) should watch the film. I mean watch it — as an audience. I even think it's a good idea to watch it *with* an audience. Maybe just an audience of a few friends — but an audience, nonetheless. It will give you a really good idea of the moments in the film where you feel uncomfortable because it drags, or the part where you thought people would laugh — and it's deathly quiet — or worse yet, where people laughed and it was supposed to be serious…umm, okay, so *that* didn't work.

Especially note those parts where you feel you *have to explain what's going on*. Not good.

Take notes while you're watching with that audience so you know *exactly* where it didn't work. I promise you, if you do this you won't have that *very* uncomfortable feeling of seeing your finished film with an audience for the first time at a festival and having them laugh at *all the wrong places*. Or worse, having them laugh when it's not supposed to be funny! Better to have that happen with close friends or family and then fix it when you're still in the editing phase.

Now, go back to your editor and fix those parts. Either take out the scenes that don't work or tighten them up. In my experience, most first-time filmmakers err on the side of making their project too long. The scenes are too long, the project is too long—the rhythm just isn't right. If you or your director can't *feel* the rhythm of the scene, get someone who can. If you're doing a comedy this is *especially* important as rhythm in comedy will make or break your project. If you get it wrong here it will never, and I mean *never*, be right or funny. You need to get it right. Everything you do beyond this is going to hinge on a cut that is locked. So, getting a final cut of the project that you love, that *feels* right and that has the right rhythm to it is imperative.

If you need to do this part several times (meaning edit, screen, fix, and then repeat that process) then do it. I can't stress enough that when you *lock picture* you can't go back and change it. Oh, well, yes you can. But it will become increasingly more difficult to do—and more costly—because your composer and your sound are all going to do *their* work to a locked picture with time code. So any change, even one frame, will throw that time code off. They'll have to adjust what they're doing and it will cost you more money. So take the time you need to get it *just right* before you move on. Make sure you *love* that film *without* music or sound fixes before you move on. If you do, I promise you, you'll love it even more *with* the music and sound fixes.

One thing I would caution against: don't let your editor cut to a temp track (temporary music track). You and your director will be hearing that track over and over as you watch the film materialize. You'll either grow to love it, or hate it, and you'll *never* be able to use it. Never. It will be too expensive or you won't be able to clear it. Cut the film dry. As you watch the film materialize, let the film tell you what kind of music you want to hear.

Second, and probably more important, if you cut your film to music you'll never actually *know* which scenes don't work. Yep. I said it. If the rhythm of the scene is off or the scene isn't working, for whatever reason, the music will cover it up. The emotion or feel of the music will take over and make the scene *feel* like it works. Better to cut the film dry to see and feel where it's off, and fix it. Let the music enhance a film that works instead of cover up a film that's flawed. If your editor insists on cutting to music, either get a different editor or have him turn off the music track when you watch together so you can see it without the music track. It should enlighten him, too.

My life has taught me one lesson, Hugo, and not the one I thought it would.
Happy endings only happen in the movies.

—Hugo, 2011
Martin Scorsese, dir

12: The Score

I usually go to music next because it can take awhile for the composer to write their score and get it just right. So, once I have a locked picture—and not before—I send the picture to my composer. I have someone that I work with on pretty much everything I do. Maybe you'll find someone like that for your projects, too. There are plenty of composers out there who want to work. Audition them. Listen to their reels. Once you have your locked picture your director will probably have a pretty good idea of what style of music will suit the film best. She may want to talk it over with you—since you are the producer after all—and you may also have a definitive idea of what style of music you hear in the piece as well.

Don't just go for songs performed by a band. I also wouldn't advise going with wall-to-wall music, either. A film or web series that has music playing throughout the entire film just screams of amateur filmmaking. Music is meant to enhance the story and the visuals, helping to augment the emotional impact, not cover anything up. In fact, some of the most beautiful, eloquent moments in film have been in total silence, where the music and sound track just laid out completely.

If you aren't familiar with much in the way of music, start listening to film scores. Notice how the different instruments evoke different feelings. See which instruments evoke what specific feelings for you. How do the strings make you feel? What about the lower strings—like a cello? What about the horns? Do trumpets make you feel different than a French horn? How about guitars? Does an acoustic guitar evoke a different feeling for you than an electric guitar? You *can* just hand your piece over to the composer and let them run with it. Many composers are good enough to create something that you'll be happy with. Since I write and direct most everything that I produce (and since I began my career in music) I become very involved in this process—telling the composer exactly what style of music and which instruments I want to feature. Don't be afraid to tell the composer exactly what you want if you have something specific in mind. That helps narrow the field for them (just as having that list back at the beginning helped to narrow the field for you as a writer).

Oh and if you watch lots of movies, as I do, and you watch classic movies, old movies, good movies and bad movies—all with the idea that you can learn from everything you see—you may come to the same conclusion that I have, which is that classic movies, the ones that always seem timeless no matter when they were made, almost always have a classical score—a musical score that is grounded or inspired by classical music. The movies that have 'music of the day' or a musical score that is inspired by the musical styles that were popular in that decade, be it the 30s the 70s or the 90s, seem dated when I watch them now. If you want your movie (or web series) to have that timeless quality, I would caution you to lean toward music that is inspired by classical music and not the music that is popular today, whenever *today* happens to be.

One other thing about music—there are people out there who call themselves composers, but all they're really doing is putting a synth pad under the visuals. It just sounds like chords that are changing…one after the other. To me, that just isn't composition. To me, composition is writing musical themes…melodies that evoke a feeling. Now that feeling might be majestic, angry, bitter, melancholy, humorous, quirky…it could really be anything. A theme, a melody can evoke a feeling and create an identity for your piece more than changing chords. So look for a composer who actually writes music. Yes, a tense moment will most likely have an unresolved, tense chord (not a melody). However, most movies, whether they be SciFi, drama, action, comedy, horror or RomCom will have moments where we identify with our Protagonist and that heroine (or hero) will have a melodic 'theme' that is recognizable. That is a melody – not a synth pad or chord. If your composer can't write interesting, compelling melodies then they're not really a composer.

Are you not entertained?! Are you not entertained?!
Is this not why you are here?

—Gladiator, 2000
Ridley Scott, dir.

13: Sound and Sound FX

At the same time that my composer is writing the score I have a sound designer working on the sound. "Why do you do that?" I'm often asked. "Didn't you get good sound on location?" Well, yes...and no. If you have a sound guy recording sound during production you should get good sound. Period. However, all the sound effects will not necessarily be picked up by his microphone. In fact, some of them are *purposefully* not picked up by the microphone, or even recorded *at all*. "Like what?" you ask. For instance: the ringing of a phone; the buzzing of a text message; footsteps as they walk around, in and out of the room; the knock on the door; birds in the park; the lonely wind in the mountains. In fact, there are so many things it *could* be, that it's difficult to imagine what it might be for your project. All I can say is that a good post-production sound designer will watch your movie and will see and hear everything that should be there and isn't. Then they'll put those sounds in—perfectly in sync. It's called foley, it's an art and what a difference it makes. Suddenly your slightly amateurish project takes on the most professional proportions.

Here's what I know: many self-producers aren't paying any attention to post-production sound. It's not because they don't care—they just don't hear what a sound designer hears. They got a good sound guy to get production sound and they figure they've done their job. The problem here isn't neglect, it's ignorance, because production sound is only about 25% of the sound that really needs to be there.

If you spend just a little more money in post and hire a sound designer, your project will sound much more professional. Oh, and that noise, that hum in the background of the scenes that sounds kind of bad? Most sound designers have really cool equipment and software that can get rid of that in a snap. Here's a suggestion: try hiring one of these guys right out of film school. They'll have experience working on projects in school but most likely want to get professional experience and credits and will work on your project for less money to get those credits.

If you're doing a short film or a web series for serious award consideration (we'll discuss this more in Industry Recognition) I definitely suggest getting post-production sound design. However, if you're just shooting a scene for your reel or your first project you can probably get away with having your editor source most, if not all of the sound effects you'll need. He may not even have to pay for them as there are some sites out there where these sounds effects are available for free. But if he does have to pay, it's really a nominal amount. And many of the editing programs now have very sophisticated sound modules that can remove the hum and hiss of the background noise that sometimes is found on the soundtrack as well. Be sure to ask your editor if she can do this for you.

You had me at 'hello.'
—Jerry Maguire, 1996
Cameron Crowe, dir.

14: Color Correction

Okay, by now you're probably saying to yourself, "Really, Kathi?! You've gone too far!!" Look, you don't have to do color correction on your project. If you had a good DP, shot with a good camera and had a good gaffer (light guy) your footage is probably pretty well matched. However, you may have a scene, here or there, where the color is a little green or the lighting is a little darker than you'd like. Maybe you had to shoot the same scene over a couple of different days — and the scene was outdoors — and one day it was sunny and the next day it was cloudy. Uh oh! Those pieces won't match when cut together. Unfortunately, this happens — especially on low-budget projects. It may be something that you, as a less experienced filmmaker, don't see until the film is cut together. On my film, *Worth*, we only had one scene where we did any color correction. One scene. But every film is different.

If your editor is skilled, they should be able to adjust those things for you in their editing program. Otherwise, you'll want to hire someone who has that skill and have them do something called "color correction." Basically this means taking any scene where you want the color or exposure adjusted and they do that, being careful to make sure that each one of the shots and angles matches the others. It requires skill and a good eye, is a little painstaking, but it will make your project look so much better.

You can't believe how many films I've seen at film festivals that were shot on a RED camera, where the exposure was blown out, overexposed and/or the scenes had a yellow cast to them. This was not done on purpose or as a stylistic choice, mind you. Either the filmmakers didn't know what they were doing when they shot the film or they didn't take the time to do color correction. Either way it just looks amateurish. Also, as you'll discover when we get to Distribution (Chapter 11), if you want your project to stand out and get attention for you, you're going to have to do better than that.

Well, here's another nice mess you've gotten me into!
— Sons of the Desert, 1933
William A. Seiter, dir.

15: The Mix

At this point you've taken the time and trouble to have some of your sound issues fixed and cleaned up, and added some sound effects (foley) to your project and you've had a music score written. Awesome and well done! Now you have to mix all that sound. Whaa???

Yep. The sound all needs to be mixed together in order to achieve a balanced level of sound. You want to be able to hear the dialogue above the music and sound effects and you want the levels of music and effects to be just right, relative to each other, in order to produce just the right emotional impact.

Music Mix

The first thing I'm going to talk about is a music mix. If all your music was done on a computer, you won't need this—your composer will have done his own mix before he outputs the final file for you.

Here's where I do things a bit differently for my projects. I work with a composer who agrees with me that, at least for my bigger (and more important) projects, a live instrumental sound along with the computer creates the feel of live musicians—it gives the audience the idea that more of the music was created with an orchestra and not just on a computer or synthesizer. So, he takes one (or two) of the main instruments and hires a live player to record that part in a studio. It costs a little bit more, and it requires a music mix.

However, it sounds *so much better* than just a computer score that I've come to insist upon it almost every time.

The music mix is done by someone who knows what they're doing and has the proper equipment and set-up to do this. I'm sure your composer will know someone who is capable. What you'll be listening for is the smooth integration of the live musician(s) with the computer-generated music.

Overall Mix (or Dub Mix)

Once you have your music score mixed (which may or may not apply to your project), it's time to do an overall mix. If you want a 5.1 surround sound final output (because you'll be screening in a theatre with surround sound) you'll want to do this in a 5.1 surround sound theatre that's fully calibrated. If you just want a stereo mix you can do it in a smaller theatre. In any event, if this is a *film*, I recommend doing your mix in a theatre on the theatre speakers. On my first film we did the mix in a studio, listening to it on studio speakers, and then at the first screening *in a theatre* with an audience we were very surprised to hear that the music overpowered the dialogue in the second half of the film. Yikes!! Not good. We had to go back and re-mix, which cost more money. Better to spend a little more money in the beginning, do your mix in a theatre and get a good first mix, than to have to go back.

If, however, you're mixing a web series a studio will do just fine since people will be watching it on their computers at home, or on their handheld devices. It all depends upon what the final output will be—where people will be watching your project.

The purpose of the mix is to establish the relative levels of the dialogue, the sound effects and the music. This is definitely a subjective thing and your director, mixer and composer will all want to be in attendance. You should be there, too. Many ears will make for the best mix. You can all weigh in on what sounds best to you thereby getting the best mix for each scene. Be prepared to spend many hours on this process as you go over and over each scene—and sometimes moments within the scenes themselves—in order to get them just right.

You should also note that, in terms of sound, the guys who work on post-production sound have specialties. This means that the sound *designer*—the one who adds in the sound effects—specializes in doing that and doesn't necessarily specialize in mixing sounds. You'll most likely need to find a different person to do the mix.

One of the many things that you'll want to do as you mix the sound is to adjust the levels for maximum emotional impact. What do I mean? Well, just watch some movies. You'll note that in some scenes the dialogue will start and then it will fade away as the music swells, taking over completely. That was done in the mix. Or, in the alternative, the music may be playing to a climactic point and then just drop out to silence as the two characters whisper their revelatory moment of dialogue to each other. That, too, was accomplished in the mix. Both of these are an example of how sound, music and dialogue can be manipulated, in the mix, for maximum emotional impact. Once you realize that this is part and parcel of how movies are made, you'll start watching and listening very differently, but you'll also know how to use this tool yourself.

Once you're finished with the mix, you will end up with a single sound track and a single picture track that join together via a sync mark, put onto the film and the soundtrack by the editor. This sync mark is placed onto the film right at the very beginning, just before the opening title sequence. At this point your project is done.

NOTE: If you're working on a web series, you may decide to forego some of these steps, deciding that you don't need quite as sophisticated sound as a film (especially if you're only releasing it on the internet). In that case, your editor may be able to clean up any sound issues you have in his/her editing program and add any sound effects you need, and do a simple mix in their editing software, marrying the music with the sound right there. You'll need an experienced editor, but it can be done.

FINAL NOTE: If you're doing a feature and you want Dolby sound and you hope to sell your feature for some type of distribution, be aware that you'll need an official Dolby studio to do your calibration as Dolby will want to certify that it was done to their specifications before they will let you buy a licensing agreement. That licensing agreement is part of the "deliverables" that you will have to provide to the distribution company.

Your ancestors called it magic, but you call it science.
Well, I come from a place where they're one and the same.

—Thor, 2011
Kenneth Branagh, dir.

Part Five: Distribution

*Sawyer, you're going out a youngster,
but you've got to come back a star!*

—42nd Street, 1933
Lloyd Bacon, dir.

16: Marketing

Now *this* is where you'll decide just how to put your project into the public eye and awareness. Marketing is so important that you *could* hire someone just for this.

The first thing you'll want to do is establish a brand or logo for your project. This usually is the poster or online image that people will come to associate with your project. How to do that? Well, I will tell you — it's easy and it's not, all at the same time (hmm, a recurring theme here, yes?).

If you crafted a project around *your* brand, and you did it well, it shouldn't be too difficult. Here's the first rule: whatever emotion you want your project to evoke in your audience, your poster should evoke that emotion just by looking at it. Say what? Did that even make sense?

Okay, let me break it down. Let's say you've produced a comedy web series. Okay. Easy enough to understand, right? When people watch the episodes, you want them to laugh. Still with me? Okay. So, when people look at the poster — you want them to smile, maybe even chuckle a little. You see, it evokes a little of the same emotion that the episodes evoke. The poster lets us know that we'll feel that laughter emotion — that we'll *want to laugh* or feel inclined to laugh — when we watch the episodes because we have already started down that emotional pathway just by looking at the poster.

If you start looking at movie posters you'll notice that the good ones do this. A comedy will have something funny on the poster — something that makes you smile. A drama will have something dramatic on the poster — something that seems sad or dark or mysterious, depending on which end of the drama spectrum they're going for. An action film will usually have some action elements on the poster—like an explosion or a gun or a chase scene. A love story will usually have two people locked in an embrace or a look that says, "I love you." The poster hints at what's to come in a provocative way—in a way that makes you think and *feel*.

This is what you want to do as well. You want to hint at what's to come. You want to take the elements of what you've written, produced and created and give the audience a *tease*—evoke a little bit of the emotion that the audience will feel when they watch your piece—and intrigue or fascinate them. You want to create something that makes the audience think about what you're serving up but doesn't answer all their questions. A good piece of marketing will do all that. A bad piece of marketing will do none of that. It will just be a picture of the lead or will have nothing to do with the project. It will confuse the audience.

Adding a tag line that elucidates what's going on or hints further at the mystery (or the comedy or the drama) can also add to the marketing of your project. Marketing departments are paid huge sums of money to produce these elements. Unless you can afford to hire someone you're going to have to figure these things out on your own.

You can do it if you get creative.

What I suggest is you look at what other successful ad campaigns have done. Don't steal, but *be inspired* by them. So, if you've created a short film that is an action piece, go find three other really successful action features that are similar to yours in style and tone and look at their posters online. Google them. See what those posters look like. They're probably all somewhat similar to each other. What are the elements that comprise those posters? Which of *those* elements do you have in your film? How can you compose a poster, with the elements that you have in your film that may be similar in style or layout to their posters but evokes the action and story of *your* film? Use their poster as a guide and inspiration, but be original—your poster should tell the story of your film.

Here let me caution you: less is more! Keep your poster and marketing materials uncluttered. If you study the marketing materials put out by the big studios you'll note that they are generally clean and simple. Yours should be, too. The more stuff you have on your poster the more it looks like a B movie or lower-budget fare. Always strive to have your project look more upscale.

If you're doing a web series you may not want to do a full-fledged movie-style poster, but you'll definitely want to produce what would be considered the brand artwork—or poster artwork for the series. It's really the same type of thing, just not necessarily in the exact size and layout of a movie poster. Go online and look at the different web series in your genre and see what kinds of artwork they have on their homepage at their website. What size and format is the layout in? Do they have a tag line? Or just the title and the artwork?

If you're a creative person this will actually be fun!! It can start the wheels turning about your project—honing in on the genre and how best to capture your unique story points on the poster. Experiment. Try different things. Don't expect to get it right the first time. You'll *know* when you get it right. It will suddenly all snap into place and look just right, and people will respond to it.

If this isn't your cup of tea then find someone who likes doing this and have them try some things for you—this can become someone you add to your team. Brainstorm with them until they have the full picture of the project and can start putting some things together for you.

Okay, now you have your marketing materials—let's get this puppy out there!!

17: Distribution Outlets

Web Series and Scenes

I'm going to group these two together as the mode of distribution for them both is online.

For your scenes, you're either going to just put them up on a YouTube channel that you create (your own branded channel, hopefully) or, if they're comedy scenes, you could try putting them on Funny or Die.

If it's a web series, with multiple episodes, you can also put it up on a YouTube channel of your own (or Funny or Die), you could create your own website around the series or you could try submitting your material to one of the various distribution outlets out there. There are several and I won't list them all here as more are added (and some go away) all the time. Suffice it to say as you do your research you'll find that different channels cater to different genres and styles of material, so you will want to make sure that you submit appropriately, if that's the route you choose to take.

Please be aware that whatever outlet you choose, whether you create your own channel or website or you choose to place your content at one of the existing channels out there, you will need to drive people to it—meaning *you* will need to do a lot of marketing to get people to visit and watch. We'll be reviewing how to do that in Chapter 18.

Here's the thing that I have stressed from the beginning: doing your project professionally and taking the time, money and care to do the best job you can is going to pay off and here is where the payoff happens. Understand that the market is saturated, and I mean *full* of creative people who are producing projects for themselves. You are not the only actor who got the brilliant idea to self-produce. With the proliferation of high-definition cell phone cameras, inexpensive DSLRs, other HD cameras and the fact that you can edit now on a laptop, it can seem like everyone has become a filmmaker. Although not technically true, I think that's great because it evens the playing field. What does that mean for you? It means you should do your best work and put it out there. If you do that—if your work is executed at a higher level than the masses or there is something unique and different about it—it will stand out. It will stand out just by virtue of the fact that you've created something of quality, something that people relate to and something from your heart.

That old expression "cream rises to the top" has never been more appropriate than right now. Projects produced with care and quality stand out. Those that are truly unique and original, not just a rehash of someone else's ideas, will stand out—especially if they arise from a heartfelt passion.

Not only will your project stand out to the general public, but it will also stand out to those who are selecting projects for their networks—the various Internet (and broadcast) channels that decide what programming to select. So, you stand a better chance of being selected for that prestigious Internet channel if you produce something truly distinctive and do it well.

Finally, your project—and you—will stand out to the buying public: those people that you want to see *you* acting in a web series and turn around and hire you for their TV series or film. This is, after all, why you did this in the first place, right?

Short Film

If you produce a short film you can either put it online or you can enter it into film festivals. If you want to enter it into film festivals I would caution you to *not* put it online initially, however, as many festivals have a rule against films that have been available online and will not accept them. Now, that 'rule' is changing and relaxing as we become a more digital world, but I would still advise you to do some research, keep your film offline at first and then, when you know you've done your festival run to all the places that care about that sort of thing, go ahead and post your film. There will always be time to put it online.

Here are my secrets to getting your film into film festivals:

Understand that there are tiers of festivals, just like there are tiers of actors, directors, producers and everything else in this business. There are the A festivals—those international festivals where winning the top prize can qualify your film for entry into competition for the Academy Awards: Sundance, Clermond-Ferrand, Cannes, Berlin, Palm Springs, Santa Barbara, San Francisco International, etc.—and some that won't qualify for that top prize but are still quite prestigious: Tribeca, SXSW, Stonybrook. Then there are 'just under' the A festivals—those that are also prestigious, but perhaps not quite as prestigious as an A festival: Phoenix, Sedona, Rochester International, Los Angeles Shorts, Ojai, Festroia, WorldFest Houston. There are B level festivals and C level festivals—small local festivals. These festivals are still somewhat picky, but since they don't get as many submissions as the bigger fests they will accept a film with less production quality or one that has no name actors. (N.B. just because I've listed or *not* listed a festival here doesn't mean it is/is not included in the 'A' tier. With a few exceptions, the hierarchy of festivals can change from year to year.)

The first thing to understand is this: the field is glutted with people producing short films. This is the easiest—and least expensive—form of film to produce, therefore it is the most competitive category in film festivals. There are hundreds and/or thousands of short films competing for a handful a slots at any particular festival (depending on the festival) so your film has to be better than 80-90% of what's out there *just to get accepted into a festival*. If you want your film to be selected at film festivals the first criteria is to produce something of quality. Take care in the execution of your product. For example, when my film WORTH qualified to be eligible for Academy consideration, there were only 66 films in that small pool. This year there were 140 films that qualified for Academy consideration.

Second: Research, research, research. Not every film is right for every festival. The cardinal mistake I see almost every short filmmaker make is to submit their film to Sundance. Sundance has a particular appetite. They favor a certain type of film. Figure out what that is. If your film doesn't fit into that genre or style then don't waste your money. Also, note that if their programmers change, then that type of film may change, too.

Let me add here, if you didn't start out by answering one of those first two questions, "I want to make a short film that gets into Sundance," then why would you even waste your money? Or, by the same token, if you didn't answer one of the questions: "I want to make a short film that gets nominated for an Academy Award," then why would you *only* submit to Academy-qualifying festivals? Short films that either (a) get accepted to Sundance or (b) get nominated for an Academy Award are very narrow in their scope and qualifications. If *that* is what you want to do, I suggest you research exactly what genres, budgets, and other criteria are used for judging at those two venues and craft your project accordingly. Then you will have a better chance at achieving what you desire.

Every film festival has a type of film that they like. It's pretty easy to figure out what that is. It just takes time and painstaking research: you go to the festival website online, see what films were selected and which ones won Best Short Film and/or Audience Favorite for the previous year or two. Then Google those films. Each one of those films ought to have a trailer online—whether on their own website or on Youtube or

Vimeo. Heck, they may even have the entire film online. Once you've watched the film (or the trailer) you can see whether or not it's similar to yours in terms of style, quality of execution, genre, tone, etc. If so, then this festival is probably a good fit for your film. If not, it doesn't mean that your film definitely would *not* be accepted there, just that the chances are less likely. If it's a festival that you really, *really* want to try for, go ahead and try. Otherwise, spend your money on festivals where the chances are more in your favor.

Lastly, I'm going to state this here: if you didn't start out at the beginning of this producing journey answering those two questions back from Chapter 2 (why did you do this and what do you want to have happen because you did) then… it's going to be a rough road here. I cannot tell you how many filmmakers I run into who make a film, screen it right before they go out onto the festival circuit and ask for some advice about where they ought to go with it and my first question is, "What do you want this to accomplish for you?" When they look back at me with a blank stare, I then ask them why did you do this film in the first place? I usually get an answer like, "Well, I was bored," or "I was just looking to do something," or sometimes no answer at all. This is no way to pursue a career in producing or directing. Without a clear vision of why you're producing something I'm not sure how I can now suggest where it ought to go.

Okay, back to film festivals. Now, what I've outlined above is the economy method of film festival submission. If you're of the mindset that time is money and would rather use what I call the scattergun approach, then by all means go ahead. In this approach, particularly with your first film, submit to all the festivals that suit your fancy. Any and every festival that sounds interesting to you. You will come to find out the ones that have an inclination toward your style by the acceptances that you receive and can start to narrow your submissions accordingly. Then, when you venture onto the festival circuit with your second, third and fourth film, you have your list of the festivals you will target first. It doesn't mean that you won't add to that list and, perhaps, drop some off the list as your filmmaking skills become more proficient.

One of the perks of being a repeat filmmaker on the circuit (and of actually going to the festivals and getting to know the programmers and the festival directors) is that the second, third and fourth time around you can often get discounted, or free submissions, based on your previous screenings and awards at their festivals. For some festivals this is a stated policy. For others, it doesn't hurt to ask.

There are festival clearing houses, detailed in the Appendix. Go there, check out the many film festivals worldwide, and figure out which interface you feel comfortable working with and which festivals are right for *your* film.

If your film is a first-time effort, produced on a modest budget (5-figure or below) with no name actors in it, I'm going to suggest that you start off by submitting to what I call B or C level festivals—local or regional festivals that won't be attracting the more expensively-produced films with 'name' talent attached. Don't get precious about this—everyone has to start somewhere. There is no rule that says you're going to start at the top and get your first film into Sundance, Tribeca or SXSW. I have a friend who produced/directed her first short film and *only* submitted it to Academy-qualifying festivals. Period. Instead of consulting me, she went ahead and spent all her money submitting the film to the top tier *only*. Not that her film was bad. It was quite good; particularly for a first effort. But I knew when I saw it that it most likely would *not* be accepted into many, if any, of the Academy-qualifying festivals. I've been to those festivals with my films. I know the caliber of films that they accept, and they're looking for the cream of the crop, worldwide.

Decide early on if this is a one-time thing for you or if this is something you want to pursue as a career. If so, you'll want to develop a relationship with the programming directors at the various festivals so that when you submit your films to them, year after year, they'll be more inclined to take them. If you decide this is something you want to continue to do, then I recommend carefully choosing your festivals with that in mind, knowing that you'll want to travel to as many of them as possible in order to meet and interact with the festival directors and build relationships with them, as well as participate and partake in everything that the festival has to offer.

Going to festivals and seeing your film with an audience is something I cannot recommend enough. It is one of the perks of having gone through this process. This is when you really get to have fun, meet other filmmakers, see many films and learn about the filmmaking process from the outside in. You can network, attend panels (even participate in some) as well as screen your film and participate in the Q&A that inevitably follows. Don't be nervous about that—you'll do fine. People just want to know how and why you came to make your movie!

Third: Understand that submitting to, and being accepted to screen at, film festivals is a numbers game. If your film is very, very good, you'll still only be accepted to screen at somewhere between 30-50% of the festivals to which you submit. That's just the way it works. So, decide in advance how many festivals you want your film to participate in (and how many you can afford to submit to and/or attend), and then go through the thousands out there and pick the ones you most want. For instance, if you'd like your film to screen at 12 festivals, then I'd suggest you submit to at least 25-30 and hope for the best. You may wind up submitting to *more* than that in order to reach your 12 and, as things go, you may get lucky and submit to 30 and screen at 15 or 20. YAY you!!

Fourth: Yes, submitting to film festivals *can* be pricey if you look at it as one big chunk. But here's the secret to saving money and having a better chance of your film being selected:

submit on the earlybird cycle. *Always*. If you miss it by ONE DAY, wait until next year. Why? Well, first of all, they have these film festivals every year. They're not going to close down after this year and your film isn't going away. So relax and know that you have time to do this right. Second, when you submit on the earlybird cycle you save money. I know, it only looks like a little—sometimes as little as $5 to $10—but added up over 10-12 festivals, that can be well over $100. Add it up over 50 festivals and that can be over $500. See how quickly that adds up?

Here's another thing—and this may be even *more* important: during the earlybird cycle the festival selection people are fresh and excited about seeing new films. It's been months since they held their previous festival and they're raring to see some new films and pick them out for the next festival. They're hoping to see some good ones and they're hoping yours will be one that they'll like. If they *do* like yours it goes into the pile of "We like these and want these in the festival." In fact, they start building their programs around the ones they select early in the cycle. If you wait and submit later in the cycle your film had better be really, really spectacular in order to (a) knock someone else's film out of the running; or (b) make them decide to change a program that they've already started putting together; or (c) fit into a pre-existing program they've already started building. See how that works?

You're probably thinking, "Wait, Kathi, if everybody reads this book then aren't they all going to be submitting on the earlybird cycle and then this advice won't work anymore—the screeners will be inundated with films early in the cycle." I suppose if thousands of people read this book and everyone took my advice at the same time that would be true. But realistically, I can't imagine everyone reading this will actually take my advice and not all at the same time. Oh, and everyone won't submit to the same film festivals, right?

Whew! Good! 'Cause I might want to produce another short film some day, too, you know. ;-)

When I started, years ago, I would send a DVD screener to the festivals for consideration, printed with the poster art from the film right on the disc. Today Film Freeway offers the option of uploading your film and sending an online screener for free. On Film Freeway you can either upload your screener directly to the site or link to a private Vimeo link (with password). So the future is here and, at this point, the DVDs will only be used when the festivals request them as screeners (BTW, as this book goes to print it has been announced that WAB will be shutting down and no longer operating as a film festival submission site by the end of the year. This is really the end of an era as they were the granddaddy of film festival submission sites for, literally, years! So any information in this book about Without a Box will soon become obsolete. That's how fast things can change in this business. Whew!)

In the Appendix I give you a list of several of the different film festival submission outlets, and there are more opening each year. Decide which one works for you. Some people liked the fact that WAB had a large selection of festivals, both in the U.S. and abroad and, because they were owned by Amazon, once your submission was received by an 'approved' festival your project was listed automatically on IMDb. Other people like the fact that Film Freeway allows them to submit with their own, password-protected, full-HD Vimeo link. Many people want to start with foreign festivals because a number of those festivals do not have a submission fee. There are several portals that cater specifically to the foreign fests. However, be aware that foreign festivals are much more difficult to get an acceptance for a U.S. film than U.S. festivals. There are so many choices, it's really up to the individual filmmaking team how they want to proceed.

Now, a final note: if you are particularly ambitious and decide to produce a feature, be aware that if you want to sell it into distribution you'll be required to provide what are called 'deliverables.' Those include: specs, music cue sheets, EDL (edit decision list), contracts for cast and crew, subtitles, closed captions, licensing agreements, etc. This is not to scare you off but to make sure that you keep track of all these things along the way, or have a good line producer. Even when I put my short films on TV I was required to provide the music cue sheets (and licensing agreements) as well as releases (if any) for product names that might be visible in the frame.

If I'm doing a fake movie, it's gonna be a fake hit.

— Argo, 2012
Ben Affleck, dir.

18: So Who's Going to See It?

That's the big question, isn't it? Who is going to actually *see* your project? When I wrote about marketing in Chapter 16 I really only spoke about putting together the poster or the marketing *materials* for your project—I didn't go into the details of what to do with them or how to 'get the butts in the seats,' so to speak. So lets address that here.

Online

First, for your online audience, there's nothing like starting with a big following. Do you have an online presence? Do you Twitter? Do you Facebook? Pinterest? Blog? Instagram? If you don't or if you aren't already doing something on social media *regularly* I'm going to encourage you to 'pick your poison' and start; get really active with one. I don't really think it matters which one you choose, so you shouldn't force yourself to do something you just don't jive with. I also don't think you need to do *everything*. So, if Twitter isn't your thing, then don't do it. If you just can't speak your mind in 280 characters or less and you really want to stretch out and write about what's going on in a longer format, perhaps blogging is for you. If you prefer saying it with pictures—perhaps Instagram or Snapchat will be your thing.

What I'm trying to say here is you need to step out and let the people who share your interests and passions find you. This is really what social media is all about—it's about finding your audience, letting them find you and connect with you. Your audience will be those people who are interested in the same things that you are interested in and who are, therefore, interested in *you*. Those people will find you online through one of these outlets if you start participating. Speak your mind. Put your opinions out there. Engage with other like-minded people. Before you know it you'll have friends or followers who like what you stand for, who like what you like and who engage with you. This is your core audience—your fans—and these are the people who will be interested in what you put online—whether it be on your Youtube channel or on a more formal format, like Funny or Die, Koldcast TV[xii], Blip TV[xiii] or one of any number of channels available to program your material.

You'll also want to put out a press release. Once you're ready to release your project, write a press release. Okay, "how do I do that?" you're asking yourself. First, read some of the sample press releases in the Appendix so you understand what a press release looks and reads like. Then you go to one of the free online PR sites like PR Log[xiv] or Max-It Magazine[xv] where you can publish for free.

The distribution options out there are not limited. Consider entering your web series into a film festival—there are many film festivals that take web series. Another option is to enter yourself or your other lead(s) into the Emmy® FYC – even a nomination could go a long way to getting eyeballs on your show (I talk extensively about this in Chapter 20). You just need to do your research and figure out what kind of publicity and awareness you want for your web series or film.

Film Festival

When you get accepted to screen at a film festival you receive notification from the festival, usually by way of email. Awesome! Now the work begins. Many people just sit on their laurels at this point and let the festival do all the work—meaning make the festival get the butts in the seats and promote their film. Yes, the festival *is* going to get an audience and promote the films—but they're going to promote all the films, not just yours. My suggestion is to get busy and promote your film, along with the festival, so you can get more people out to actually *see* your film!

So, what should you do to promote your specific film in that festival? There are several things you can do.

The first thing you want to do is write a press release detailing a specific, interesting and press-worthy thing about your film and, of course, noting that it has been accepted to screen at that particular festival. This lets the press know exactly when and where that screening will take place (you will be given this information from the festival). You will want to put that press release out on the internet at the free press release sites I listed.

You can also promote your film in the area that's local to the festival. Some film festivals will give you their press contacts, if you ask (and yes, you often have to ask). Simply send them an email, letting them know that you are adept at doing PR and marketing for your film and would like to promote the fact that it is screening at their festival. Of course, emphasize the fact that you will be promoting their festival, along with your film. If they give you their press contacts, that's great!! Now you put together a mailing list, making sure you "BCC" (i.e., hide) all the email addresses when you hit 'send' so it doesn't annoy the receivers, and off it goes. I always like to send my press release as a .pdf attachment or, better yet, link to it — put it in a press section on my website — and write a nice cover letter. Keep the cover letter short but sweet and let them know that you're linking them to a press release about the fact that your film is screening at the upcoming festival, that you will be attending the festival and will be available for comments or interviews during those dates (only do this if you *are* going to be attending the festival).

If the festival won't give you their press contacts (and some of them won't — they hold onto them like gold), you can go ahead and create your own list. You do this by Googling to find the local newspapers, TV and radio contacts. This should give you everything you need (including e-mail addresses) to put a list together. If the e-mail addresses aren't available online, you can call the station (or paper or online source) and politely ask for their e-mail address so you can send out some press materials.

Be professional. Write something that looks and sounds professional. If you don't know how or aren't sure what that looks like, get someone to help you who knows what they're doing. Look at examples of what works and follow those. There's nothing worse than someone who's just flailing about, putting stuff out there that's amateurish and looks bad. By all means, if you just can't do it well and can't find someone who can—don't do it at all. Let the film festival promote your film. They do an awesome job. Watch what they do. Go and see how the other films promote themselves. Learn. Perhaps by the time you've been accepted at your third or fourth festival you'll be ready to tackle this part of marketing. Or perhaps never. There's no shame in not pushing your film—in letting the festival do the work. Mind you, these suggestions are just that—suggestions. These are things that have worked for me. I share them with you so that those of you out there who have the initiative, the time and the motivation to do a little bit more will have a road map of what you can do.

I have been very, very successful in receiving a lot of press for my short films at many festivals from doing just what I outlined above. Note I said I have received a lot of press for my *short films*. This is actually pretty unusual. Most reviewers and journalists don't write about short films—they concentrate on the features. But I have had articles written about my films, I have been interviewed on local television shows, local radio shows and had my trailer played on the local ABC affiliate all because I followed the advice I gave you. Now, I didn't just say "my movie is the best. You should watch it." I spent time discovering something newsworthy about my movie, something noteworthy, something unusual and different about it that could be turned into news and wrote about that. You can do that for your movie, too. Dig deep. I'm sure there's something there.

Here… let me get you started thinking about some possibilities: maybe you convinced an older, character actor to come out of retirement to play a small cameo in your film. That's newsworthy. Maybe your film is about someone who was pronounced dead and then miraculously lived to tell the tale. That's newsworthy. Take a look at the conflict of your story—your characters and what their backstory was—or the people who were involved in helping you put together your film. Somewhere in there is a nugget of interesting information that you can develop into a press release.

Understand, this is basically what a PR person would do. They would interview you about your film, about the making of your film, about the personnel involved in the making of your film, all in order to discover what little 'newsworthy nugget' is there that they could promote. So, do their job yourself. Interview yourself. Go back and really look at your project. What was the impetus to make it? What was 'the story behind the story?' What are some of the stories from the set? What are some of the stories about how it got made? Do you have any people involved who have done other films that have gone on to win awards? Did you have an interesting story about how you obtained, say, your director or your sound guy or your DP? I'm sure you have a boatload of stories about the things you went through to get the project made and things you went through along the way *getting* the project made. Amongst those stories are one or two (or more) that are interesting and newsworthy. Write about those. Write about them in an interesting way. One of those will become the focus of your first press release—'the making of' or 'the releasing of' press release.

Let me caution you not to think that your story about being an actor and deciding to take the bull by the horns and make your own project is newsworthy enough to form the basis of your press release. It's not. Not anymore. Perhaps once upon a time that was newsworthy, but nowadays actors are doing this frequently and this is no longer news. Sure, it may have been a big step for you and I appreciate and applaud that. But unless that big step involved something *more* than just "I was focusing on being an actor and decided to take my career into my own hands," find something else.

Once you're on your way and you've been accepted at a few film festivals and have had that experience of attending them (and done a few Q&As and had *those* experiences), perhaps won an award or two, or been nominated for an award or two, then *that* can become your story for the next press release. Oh, I did tell you that you'd continue to write press releases, didn't I? Yes, you will continue to write press releases as you go. All the way until you stop — stop going to festivals, that is. There will come a point when you stop. Most short films have a life of about 1-1/2 to 2-1/2 years on the festival circuit. Yours could differ, depending upon your persistence level *and* how quickly you move onto your next project. However, it seems to me, having been on the festival circuit four times now with four different projects, that many films seem to stay out there for about 2 years, give or take. The festivals themselves generally don't want a film that's older than 2 years. Some of them don't care, but many of them do, which is why I said if you miss the deadline by a week or two (or a month or two) you can always lap around the next year — but I wouldn't wait for *two* years — you might be too late by then.

Oh, and if you decide to use Film Freeway as your primary clearing house for festivals it has a handy little reminder system that will send you an email when the deadlines are approaching. By the way, there are other websites out there where you can find lots of festivals, which I list in the Appendix.

19: New Technologies

Today the shiny new thing is live-streaming, whether it be on Instagram, Facebook Life or whatever. Tomorrow, when this book is published—who knows? That's the thing about writing a book—as soon as it's published it's really old news because things are changing so fast. So, whatever the newest platforms and technologies are, they are there for you to try on, try out and experiment with as a producer. This is your playground. Take what you like about what's out there, try it, use it, discard what you don't like and keep what you do.

You don't need to become an expert in every single platform, toolset or new technology that becomes available. However, the ability to dive into a new technology and develop enough fluidity to use it, along with the traditional skills and abilities you've learned here, makes you a multi-platform producer and that's a skill that is transferrable to whatever the *next* shiny new thing is. It also makes you invaluable to whatever our industry becomes as it morphs into the future. Because our industry is changing—make no mistake about it. Television, traditional appointment TV, is becoming a thing of the past and you're here to experience this shift and change in our dynamic industry. How exciting is that? You are on the cutting edge of changes in our industry that will define it for years to come. Or those changes will be the precursor for even bigger and more sweeping changes. Who knows? In 1966 Robert F. Kennedy delivered a speech where he quoted an ancient Chinese curse that said, "May you live in interesting times." That was then but it still holds true today. All I know is what I see, and what I see is exciting—for me and for you. I hope you are excited by what you see, too.

Embrace the changes that are here with us every day and those that are coming.

Every time a new platform or tool is introduced to the market, it usually has its 'early adopters' — those who are there to pronounce the *exact right way* to use it — all the rules about how it should be done. These stories can be helpful, but more often than not they just get in your way of being creative. To really push the boundaries sometimes you need to throw away the box and use these platforms in ways they were not designed to be used. So feel free to ignore the so-called experts in whatever the new platform is and use it however you like.

However, you want to remember that you're using someone else's platform with which to create your content. Be sure to read the Terms of Service, carefully, so that you don't lose your content or the rights to it. Make sure you understand *exactly* what you're giving up if you choose to create content on someone else's platform.

The other thing to note, especially with the live-streaming platforms, is that these technologies have a 'one-time life,' meaning that they exist for a short period of time and then they are gone. For good. Unless you save your content onto your own hard drive and then upload it somewhere else. Again, this can require a commitment of time and resources that you weren't counting on when you started. So consider what the ultimate cost is in all the stages (pre-production, production, post and distribution) when considering to use a live-streaming platform — or any new technology — as they all still play an important role, unless you want your project to have a one-time life and sacrifice 99% of your potential audience.

And one last word of caution about cloud storage. Yes, I understand that this bit of new technology can be enticing — convenient, easy, and it is certainly the wave of the future as all of our apps, music, everything really wants to be stored there. I guess I'm old-school but I like knowing that I have some level of control over the storage of my stuff just in case. I've seen and heard of people losing valuable collections of original music, artwork and more when cloud storage failed. The last thing you would want, as a content creator, is to spend a ton of money and time only to have your precious web series, short film or other piece of original work lost forever due to some failure on the part of a storage system that you don't control.

Do. Or do not. There is no try.
—Star Wars: Episode V—
The Empire Strikes Back, 1980
Irvin Kershner, dir.

PART SIX:
INDUSTRY
RECOGNITION

20: Something Gold and Shiny

One of the things that comes up in the "Why are you doing this" session with many actors is: "I want to be nominated for an Emmy®" or "I want my film to be nominated for an Academy Award®." Worthy goals. Not necessarily easy, mind you, but definitely worthy. The exciting thing about these opportunities is that to some degree the qualifying is within your ability to control. The Emmys® are a self-nominating process to your peer group. The Oscars® allow nomination by way of being a festival winner at specific festivals or through a four-wall exhibition in either New York or Los Angeles. I have gone through the process for both of these so let me tell you a little bit about how to do that and what your chances are for each.

Television Academy – The Emmys®

There are really only three categories that I am aware of as I write this that a self-producing actor can submit themselves for an Emmy® in the FYC (For Your Consideration): Guest Star, Best Actor or Actress in a Short Form Comedy or Drama series and Best Short Form Comedy or Drama Series. It's possible that once this book has been published, as time goes along, there may end up being more categories as the Television Academy changes their rules and regulations regularly (sometimes yearly). But for now, these are the ones that are available for actors to submit themselves and their work.

Many people have asked me how to either (a) become a member of the Television Academy or (b) put themselves up for the FYC for Emmy® nomination in the Short Form

Comedy or Drama Series category (in other words – web series). Since I have done this myself, and joined the Academy in the process, let me tell you how I did it. First, however, let me explain that the rules can change from year to year so I would suggest going to the Academy website to read the rules for yourself:

http://www.emmys.com/academy/organization/peer-groups/performers (This is the page for the Performer category—acting. Other categories will be different.)

Currently the requirements to *join* state that you need to have 8 qualifying credits of nationally-exhibited content in a principal role within the preceding 4 years. That means that if you had a principal role in 8 episodes of a web series you created, exhibited on, say, your Youtube channel, you can apply. This also means that if you appeared in 8 episodes of someone else's web series, nationally distributed on their website or Vimeo or Youtube, you can also apply. However, be aware that if that web series is the *only* credit that you have as an actor within the last 4 years you may only be granted Associate Status. It is up to the membership committee to decide which membership status to grant. However, I wouldn't put up your nose at Associate Status. The privileges are almost the same as full Active Status – you can go to all the Emmy® events, including the Emmys themselves, you can put yourself up in the FYC for free for your first 2 video submissions, you just can't vote for the Emmys®. Oh, and the yearly fee is a bit less than Active Status (full voting status).

Okay, so how do you submit yourself in the FYC? First, you must have a qualifying web series, which means a minimum of 6 episodes with a running time of at least 2 minutes per episode. The web series must be nationally distributed (meaning vimeo, Youtube or any commercial streaming platform). Complete the form on the Academy website for your category and select your best episode. Self-produced web series must include one sample episode for vetting purposes. It must have been broadcast (or streamed) between June 1 and May 31 of the voting year. Once your application has been received for submitting your name to the FYC ballot, which is free to Academy members, you can create video for the FYC viewing platform, which is a separate application. You are not required to join the Academy to submit your work although you would have to pay an application fee to submit a ballot application if you are not a member, which fee is equal to or greater than the membership fee.

Once your name is submitted to the FYC ballot you can create video for the FYC viewing platform so your peers can see your work before voting. This requires the payment of a fee to the Academy for *each episode* that is used to create your performance sample. I recommend your performance sample be limited to just the episode for which you are being nominated, otherwise it can become quite costly.

Pick your best work (I think having a good editor help with this is essential), prepare the edited materials (again, you need someone who is familiar with *exactly* how the Academy wants it done), fill out the forms requested on the Emmy® website and hit "submit." By the way, my husband, Dave Manship is one of their preferred vendors who edits *exactly* the way they like. He even goes to speak at the Television Academy once a year to tell people how to prepare their materials. His company is EditPlus.tv.

Okay, is that it? Well, not quite. Two things: First, this year they instituted a new policy – vetting. The Emmys® is a television organization dedicated to EXCELLENCE in the field of broadcast content. The short form category is relatively new and because the barrier to entry is fairly low (6 episodes, 2 minutes, broadcast on Youtube or similar venue) the quality of submissions was not always excellent in the past. So, now all submissions for actors and shows for the short form category will go through a vetting process to make sure that those actually placed on the ballot are of sufficient quality to bear the Emmy® moniker. This harkens back to my earlier advice—do your best work and you won't have to worry about this as your work ought to make the cut, recognizing that even in the web series category you are competing against "The Walking Dead" and other network-produced short form content.

The other category that is available for to submit your own self-produced content is the short form category itself. This is where you submit your web series for consideration as the producer. Two things here: first the vetting applies to this category as well. This means that not every show will necessarily make it onto the final ballot. Only the best shows, those that the Academy feels are worthy, will make it through the vetting process. Secondly, this is a Producer submission – meaning these shows are submitted by producers from the producing peer group. So, if you are in the Producer peer group, great! If you are not, and you are only in the Actor Peer group, then you'll have to pay the fee to submit your show. Be aware that the fee for submission for Producers is substantially more than that for Actors and plan accordingly.

By the way, if you have submitted a project and it fails the vetting process, your money is not refunded. Again, I cannot stress enough – do excellent work. Do network quality work! If you don't know what that is, find a mentor who does and pay them to help you.

The third category, Guest Star, is available when you appear as a guest star on any show broadcast on network or cable. As my husband, who prepares and processes many of these for big names and utility players alike, says, "Don't expect the network or production company to submit you for these." Sometimes they do and sometimes they don't. Katherine Joosten, who was nominated three times and won two Emmys® off of videos my husband edited for her, didn't wait for the network to submit her—she hired my husband to do it for her. If you really want to take your career into your own hands you should, too.

Next: campaigning. Do you want a nomination? You know they only nominate 5 in each category, right? Well, if you want to be one of the five, then people need to vote for you. If you want people to vote for you they have to know who you are and be willing to watch your video submission. That takes a LOT of campaigning to stand out from the crowd. Postcards? Yes. Emails? You bet. The Television Academy does have rules about how you *can* promote yourself so you need to read up on them but once you know what you can and cannot do – go forth and campaign. For actors especially, a valuable and secret marketing benefit of submitting excellent work to the Emmy® FYC is that to get an Emmy® nomination you are nominated by your peers. Approximately 2600 (at the time of this writing) performers and 400 casting directors. As you can imagine, casting directors take their responsibility very seriously and I can assure you that, in my opinion, nearly all of the 400 casting directors will watch the submitted performances from the viewing platform. You could not mail enough postcards or make enough phone calls to get 400 casting directors to willingly watch your work at a cost of less than $.50 each.

A final word about the rules. This year there was a bit of a ruckus when a few actors didn't follow protocol. In their, let's call it enthusiasm for being in the mix, they walked a little outside the rules with their encouragement to others about which performances to support. A careful reading of the rules would have kept them from advocating for what the Academy considered "block voting" and these actors' submissions were pulled from competition and they were prohibited from voting, AT ALL. So, a word to the wise: carefully read the rules and be sure to follow them. All of them.

Good luck!!

Academy Award®

I know many, many people who have made short films and suddenly think, "Hey, I could be nominated for an Academy Award®." Well… yes and no. This, too, requires a little forethought and planning on your part (remember those questions back in Chapter 2?).

Okay. So how does this work? As of this writing the rules go like this: first your film must qualify. It can qualify in one of two ways: either by winning the qualifying award at a qualifying festival (the list of qualifying festivals can be found at the Academy® website here: https://www.oscars.org/oscars/rules-eligibility) or it must be theatrically exhibited either in Los Angeles or New York for a run of 7 consecutive days where the picture must appear in the theatre listing along with the dates and appropriate times. There are very precise specifications as to what formats are allowed for exhibition and you should look those up at the Academy® website as they change from year to year. For instance, when my film qualified it had to be either 70mm or 35mm *only*. Nothing else would satisfy. Now they allow a DCP exhibition, but they are very specific about what type of exhibition that has to be and how it has to be formatted and if this is important to you (and you're spending money to make it happen) you don't want to be disqualified due to some minor infraction of the rules. The exhibition requirements may, in fact, inform your choice of acquisition format and editing process so make sure all these choices support the journey to your destination.

One of the very specific rules is that a short film may *not* have been distributed anywhere in a nontheatrical form, either on VOD/PPV, DVD distribution, inflight airline distribution or internet transmission *before* the Los Angeles or New York screening. So, if you really want to qualify for this you *absolutely cannot* sell your film for distribution or put your film on the internet before you qualify. Period.

Additionally, the short film *must be* submitted in exactly the same format and be the exact same film that was either screened in Los Angeles or New York or won the qualifying award at the qualifying festival. Which means if you screened at the qualifying festival on DCP then you must submit that exact format DCP to the Academy. If you screened at a theatre in Los Angeles in order to qualify and you screened on 35mm then that 35mm print is the one that must be submitted to the Academy. Again, I would advise you to *carefully* read the rules before attempting to go through this process because although it's not necessarily difficult, it can be somewhat expensive. And good luck!

One last thing about submitting your work to either of these—it can be very exciting, especially if you become one of the nominees. I recommend, either if you become nominated in the FYC process or your film is "shortlisted" you hire a publicist who knows how to maximize the potential of these opportunities. A publicist can get you invited to all the 'right' events, seen by the 'right' people and make sure that, even if you or your project isn't a big studio project, you still get the recognition you deserve. That's their job. They are well paid for what they do, but it can pay off in *you* taking home something gold and shiny.

By the way, for the Academy Awards® the process goes a little something like this: there are the films that qualify, then they whittle them down to 10. These are the films that are 'shortlisted.' Even to have your film be one of the films that's shortlisted is an honor. Out of the 10 films that are shortlisted come the 5 that are nominated. This happens in the narrative short film category, the short film documentary category and the animated short film category.

Part Seven: Closing Words of Wisdom

This is what I believe to be true.
You have to do everything you can,
You have to work your hardest,
And if you do, if you stay positive,
Then you have a shot at a silver lining.

— The Silver Linings Playbook, 2012
David O. Russell, dir.

21: Do's and Don'ts
Or
Nuggets of Information

When I coach people or teach this class in person I like to give little helpful hints—I call them the 'Do's and Don'ts' of self-producing. It may seem counter-intuitive to put this chapter last, but I think that once you've read and digested everything I've had to say on the subject, these nuggets will make a lot of sense *and* you'll retain them a lot longer. So, ready?

Don't Produce Your 'Baby' First or The Pancake Analogy

Yep, I like to say that producing is like making pancakes—you mix up the batter, you heat up the stove and then you pour out the first one and when it comes out onto the plate it sort of looks funny. Not really round and fluffy and golden brown like a good pancake should. Sort of misshapen and awful and you throw it away. It's actually probably just fine to eat but you'd never serve it to company. By the time you get to the second or third pancake you're a pro.

It's the same with producing. When you make your first project you're going to be learning *so many things* that by the time you get through the process and come out on the other side and actually look at it, it's going to look an awful lot like that first pancake. Oh, it'll probably look okay to everyone else but to you it'll look like a disaster. You'll see all the little problems, the sound issues, the camera mess-ups—everything you could've done better. You'll remember the snafu with the location, the actor who had to be replaced at the last minute, the props that you forgot and you won't be able to see the project objectively *or* enjoy it for what it is. Don't throw it away—definitely put it out there—because no one else will see the little errors that you see.

But here's the thing: don't produce the project that you're dying to make on the first go-round. You know the one: your baby; that project that you're really in love with. Save it. Save it for Number 2 or Number 3. You want to not only love it *before* you produce it, you want to love it when it's done, too. Trust me.

Show, Don't Tell

Okay, yes, you're not the director or the writer (well…maybe you are). But this is one of those areas where if you understand this maxim then you're more than halfway home to being able to find and select *good* material and vet a good director—one who will tell the story you want to tell. Trust me on this. When you look at the script, find places where the actors and director can 'show' us what's going on instead of having the actors 'tell' us what's going on. It's much more interesting. Film and video is, after all, a *visual* medium. People tend to forget that when they're writing their screenplays and fall in love with their words. You are the person who can help them fall out of love with the words and let the camera do the talking.

As the producer it's your job to develop the material. What do I mean by that? I mean, simply, if you're not the writer then you're either hiring a writer or you're finding already-written material. In either case, it will be more than likely that you'll want some rewrites once the script is finished. If you know this maxim, it will help you to tighten up the script and make it better *before* you start production. And before you start production is where you want to do this work. It will save you so much time.

Shorter is Better—Less is More

Really. In the editing room, make it shorter. What is essential and what is filler? Cut the filler. Trust the audience to 'get' what's going on. They don't need to be hit over the head with everything—they're smart. Trust that. Start with your first cut, watch it, then make it shorter. I'm going to bet that you can cut at least 10-20% of your first cut and it will make the film better. Try it and see if I'm right.

You Can't Always Fix It in Post

Nope. Sorry. I know a lot of people who have hung their hopes on the little phrase "We'll fix it in post" and been mightily disappointed. Better to do it right, when you're shooting, than to try and fix it in post. Cheaper, too.

No Man Is An Island

At least you really don't want to be as far as filmmaking is concerned. Filmmaking is a collaborative medium. You want all sorts of creative people around you, collaborating with you on this journey. Everyone has something to offer. Even the grip, the PA and the craft services guy. You just never know where an awesome idea or solution to a problem will come from if you're open to receiving it from *anyone*. If you're trying to save money and do everything yourself—write, direct, produce, run camera, edit, craft services, compose the music, blah, blah, blah—you're an island. First of all it's going to just look ridiculous on the poster. Period. But more important than that, you want all these people around you because when it's just you pushing that rock up the hill—promoting and humping to get the project seen by people—it's really, really difficult. When you've got a whole community of cast and crew who are all pushing to get the project finished and promoting and helping you to get the project seen by their extended community of friends and family, it's not nearly so difficult. You need that audience that is attached to and attracted to those other people on your team. You need the collective energy and creativity of the team.

Go Ahead…Make My Day

If you're shooting under one of the SAG/AFTRA contracts, you'll want to make sure that you read it through and understand the terms of the contract so that you comply with it. If you have an AD, they should know the terms of the contract as well. That way you don't get dinged for meal penalties, turnaround and other miscellaneous things that could end up costing you extra. Don't expect anyone else to know these things. I had an AD who argued with me about the terms of the Short Film Agreement in the middle of a shooting day (he was wrong, I was right—I never worked with him again).

A Day Equals 24 Hours

Okay, I know that sounds really obvious. However, when you rent equipment you want to be sure to note the *exact* time you check it out. If you're on a 24-hour clock (and most of them are) you'll want to check it back in at the same time (or earlier) on the day you return the equipment *or* you'll be charged for an extra day (or half day). Yes, it does happen. Yes, it's happened to me. One hour late and you *will* be charged.

Indecision Costs

It costs you time and it costs you money. Producers make an infinite number of decisions during the course of pre-production, production and post. Most of them will be good. Some of them will be less so. Not making a decision is worse than making a bad one. I can't stress this enough. If you make a bad decision, you'll figure that out pretty quickly and you'll change course, fix it and get back on track. However, sitting in indecision — going back and forth without being able to *make a decision* — will take so much energy and focus away from what you need to be doing that it will kill your momentum. Make the decision. Don't worry if it's good or bad. It will sort itself out and at least you'll be moving in a direction.

Don't Be Afraid to Ask

Ask for anything. Ask for everything. Don't be afraid to hear the word "no" and hear it often. Because sometime in there you *will* hear the word "yes." Often when you least expect it. Often a BIG yes. Ask for things, ask for locations, ask for trades. Ask for bigger names in your cast than you think you can get. Just ask. The worst that can happen is that the answer that comes back will be "no." That's the worst. Then you go somewhere else and ask someone else. Simple as that. People expect to be asked, so ask them. This is one of the jobs of a producer. And hey, if you don't ask then you're already accepting a "no," aren't you? Try for the "yes."

Don't Take "No" For an Answer

As a producer you're now a negotiator. Act like it. Sometimes "no" is "no." Sometimes "no" is "maybe" — an excuse for you to offer something better — or offer *something*. It's up to you to figure out when "no" means "no" and when it means "let's talk." I don't know how to tell you to figure that out — experience, practice and making a few mistakes will probably be all you need. There are times when people say "no" and they really just want you to convince them of why this is a good idea for them. So do it. Then there are times when someone says "no" and they really mean "no." You'll get good at figuring out which is which and then: don't [necessarily] take "no" for an answer.

This is the best bad idea we have, sir. By far.
— Argo, 2012
Ben Affleck, dir.

22: The End is Really the Beginning

So, I've taken you through the nuts and bolts, told you some stories, hopefully given you some inspiration along the way. Are you ready to go out and produce something?

I hope that I inspired you to go forth and take some of your creative ideas and turn them into something fun, funny, scary, dramatic or romantic.

Yes, it's a lot of work. I never said it was easy. But it's a lot of fun along the way and, ultimately, very rewarding. Don't forget—you're not only creating something out of nothing, which is pretty amazing in and of itself, but you're also creating work for a bunch of people who would otherwise not have a project to work on. That is pretty dang awesome, too. You're also embarking on a path that will ultimately put you in the driver's seat with regard to your acting career. No one will be able to take that away from you. Ever.

I know many people who started out as actors, decided to try their hand at creating something for themselves and, through the process of producing their first or second project, decided they loved producing so much that they switched to producing first, acting second. I'm not saying it will happen for you, but having that control—being able to create something at will, when you want—is pretty intoxicating. As an actor, knowing that you have the ability to create projects for yourself so you're not dependent on others for work ...there's really nothing else like it in the world.

So my wish for you is that you take this information and run with it. As my friend Bonnie Gillespie says, "Have fun and don't suck."

Go forth and create! Go forth and produce!!

It's been aces.

—Dead Drop, 2012
Kathi Carey, dir.

Appendix

I. Positions and Definitions

What follows is a list of titles and jobs, and a description of the many responsibilities of the people that work on productions. It is geared less toward big-budget productions and more toward indie productions. Oftentimes, particularly on very small indie productions, more than one job is done by the same person. This may be the case on your production and that's okay. What is *not* okay is to not cover one of these positions. Every one of these jobs has to be done in order for your production to run smoothly. Even if that means that one person wears 6 hats, the duties all need to be taken care of.

Writer:

The person who wrote the story or adapted a previously written story from another source. They may also have originated the story. If they did not originate the story, that is usually designated on the script with the credit: "Story by." Once the story is conceived, the writer puts it in screenplay format, that is to say, they format it in the industry standard that you're used to seeing with the narrative portions starting on the left-hand margin and the dialogue centered on the page.

Producer:

The person responsible for bringing the project together. The person who decided that there was even going to be a project in the first place. They hire—and occasionally fire—everyone on the project, except, perhaps, the executive producer. They make sure that people are doing their job and that the project is completed on time and on budget. This person is with the project from conception through post-production. This may be the person who comes up with the initial idea—whether from reading an article, book or otherwise—and hires a writer to write the screenplay or options a screenplay or, if they're a multi-hyphenate, writes the screenplay. The producer is also a problem-solver. They anticipate problems, both during pre-production and production (and occasionally during post) and find ways to solve them or avoid them altogether.

Executive Producer (EP or Exec. Prod.):

Connected to the money through relationships or influence. This person helps get the film financed, either by knowing people with money or by attracting influential, moneyed people through their position in the community or by writing the check themselves. If you're lucky, you get an EP who has looked at the budget, spoken with the producer and line producer, understands the risks involved in the project and just lets you make the movie without input.

Line Producer:

The person who creates the budget, controls the money and how it's spent, oversees and creates the shooting schedule in concert with the UPM and the shot list which is created by the director and the DP.

Associate Producer:

These can be people who *actually* help the production or this can be a title given to people in exchange for something you want or need to get the project made. Generally, these people do *something* for the production (loan equipment, get deals for locations, introduce you to above-the-line talent), but this is often a *negotiated* credit.

Unit Production Manager (UPM):

The person who secures permits, insurance, deals with

the craft services/caterer, coordinates with police and/or fire marshals, if needed. This person handles a lot of the logistics on set—working with a lot of the below-the-line people like the production designer, the location scout (if you have one—he can act as one if you don't), hair and makeup, etc. This person knows the local community (where the grocery stores are, the gas stations, the Walmart, etc.) in case anybody needs anything, knows the local filmmaking bureaucracy and is a born negotiator who loves to save money wherever and however they can. They are also the person who tries to get freebies, like product placement, free coffee, bagels from the local shop, free bottled water, etc.. This person also *negotiates* with the owners of the various locations—if you have a location scout who procured your locations for you instead of using places from your list of assets. On a very low-budget project this job is often taken over by the Producer.

Location Scout:

This is the person who finds the cool locations where you're going to shoot your project. Now, if you've written your list of assets you may have acted as this yourself—procuring all your own locations in advance. But if you didn't, this is the person who will read the script, note where the various scenes are set, and go out and try and find locations to fit those descriptions. This person will usually present the Producer, the Director and DP with 2 or 3 different locations for each scene so that choices can be made.

Locations are chosen based on a variety of criteria, including the actual physical location of the proposed location and its proximity to other locations you have chosen, the way it looks and feels to the Director and DP and the ability to move cameras/lights and actors in and out of it. They will also be looking at power issues—is there enough juice at the location to power the lights or will they need to rent a generator? The terrain may also be a concern if you're shooting outdoors. A non-level surface makes for a much more difficult shoot and may require hand-held, steadicam or the laying of a level foundation or rails. All of these things can affect either the time or budget or both. You'll want to hire a location scout as soon as you set a start date, maybe sooner, as this person will be key to obtaining and negotiating your locations.

First Assistant Director (1st AD):

This is not a director. This is not the director's assistant. This is the person who runs the set. This person is responsible for keeping the production on schedule and making the day (i.e., shooting all the scenes and shots that were on the schedule to be shot that day). This is the person who keeps the crew (DP, camera, sound) and actors coordinated and ready to go for each take.

A good First can maintain an orderly working environment where shots are set up quickly, the crew and actors remain focused on the work, time isn't wasted yet keep it fun and light. A less-effective First runs the set like a drill sergeant, yelling and screaming to get the job done, make their day and keep the crew in line. I prefer the kind of First that keeps the set fun and light, but moving right along. But I'm going to tell you that I've had to work with several people in order to find someone who has that sixth sense and knows when people are working or starting to slack off; someone who is efficient, keeps everyone focused on the work and yet keeps the energy on the set fun and enjoyable. There are some who can keep the energy fun and enjoyable but the work just doesn't get done—unless you can keep *yourself* and everyone else going. There are also the less-fun, yell-at-the-crew types that just make the day long and almost unbearable. This is, obviously, a *very* important job on set. You won't need to hire this person until you're in pre-production and you have a director and a DP and they have started creating their shot list. How do you find a good one? Ask people. Ask lots of people. Get recommendations. Your director may have someone they like working with and may be helpful in guiding you to a First who keeps things moving and is pleasant to be around.

Director:

This is the person who's going to bring the project to life—the person whose creative vision will drive the project from pre-production through post. This is the person who will read the script and have the creative vision of the story—will quite literally see it in their head. This person knows how to tell a story, visually and through the actors on screen, in order to create the emotional impact that the writer intended and that you, as producer, want the audience to feel. He/she will be the *most* important person you hire.

A good director not only has the different character arcs in their mind and will be able to communicate with the actors in order to bring their best performance to the screen, but understands that film is a visual medium. Therefore, a good director will know that camera position and framing helps to tell their story and will work closely with their DP in shot selection. They also know that lighting and color sets the mood and will work closely with the DP in determining how each scene will be lit and what the predominant colors will be, both in costume and production design (i.e., what the set will look like) and whether or not there will be color added through filters or grading in post.

A good director also knows that moments of the story will be highlighted through the post-production process and will carefully choose different types of shots for the various scenes in order to give the editor specific choices in post-production. This is also the person who will be helping to choose precise scoring and music selection in post in an effort to maximize the emotional impact that the film will have.

A less-experienced director will let the DP plan and select the different shots, preferring only to work with the actors OR will spend all the time selecting shots and framing and spend no time at all with the actors, letting them hope for the best. A less-experienced director will give no thought to set direction, color, lighting, framing, but will just use the location as he or she finds it. A less-experienced director will have given little thought to the overall impact that the project will have.

You'll want to bring this person into the project fairly early in the process. Since it will be their vision that will guide the process from beginning to end, they really need to be one of the first people on board.

How do you find a good one? Watch people's work. Go online and look at their previous work. Go to film festivals and watch the shorts programs—see which films speak to you, which films create an emotional reaction, which films get the biggest response. Ask questions at the Q&A. Find out how the directors work and how they think—how they approach their work. Or subscribe to one of the online services that offers indie films and web series (like www.indieflix.com) and watch what they have to offer. There are also organizations like Alliance of Women Directors (www.allianceofwomendirectors.org) and Glass Elevator (www.glasselevate.com) both of which I'm a member, by the way, where their members are professional women directors. These are great places to find awesome female-identifying directors for your project. Also, DirecTV has a shorts-only channel that offers shorts content 24-hours per day. It won't be long before you'll be able to discern who knows what they're doing and who doesn't. Don't be afraid to request a reel. In your interview process award extra points to a director who brings ideas about character arc, development and relationship, tone, vision, style and look to the discussion— that shows a director who has given your project a lot of thought and one who is going to make your project so much better. Oh, and you do want to send them the screenplay or teleplay *before* you interview them.

Script Supervisor (Scripty):

The person—usually a lady—who keeps track of everything that happens in every frame of film. Period. They're looking at wardrobe, lighting, set decoration and props, keeping track of the exact lines the actors said and how and when *exactly* they handled a prop, what their wardrobe looked like, whether their coat was buttoned or open, whether their hair was parted on the right or the left—every minute detail so that it can be matched from shot to shot.

They also keep track of the 'line' and whether the DP and director are crossing it. They often have a mind-boggling memory or take really, really good notes. Nowadays, with cell phone cameras, they can (and often do) videotape every scene from Video Village so that they can match each scene to the last. It still means they have to remember things, but they can always go back to the video and check. Often the director will have a script supervisor that they have worked with before and like working with. If so, hire that person. You want to bring as many people as possible from the director's team to your project since they work together like a well-oiled machine. This means they will work quickly and be more likely to "make their days" (meaning accomplish all the shots planned in any given day) because they already have a shorthand with each other.

Video Village:

The place, just slightly removed from the set, where the monitor(s) is set up so that the director, scripty and others (meaning you, the producer) can watch each take as it's being filmed. If Video Village is close enough, headsets for sound aren't necessary. Otherwise, the viewers are wearing headsets so they can hear, as well as see, what's going on (on a monitor). This allows those who need to see what's being captured on camera (particularly you, scripty and the director) an unobstructed view. Oftentimes the set itself is tight—with set pieces, cameras, lights and the actors and crew—and there just isn't room for extra bodies in there. Although, as a director myself, I prefer to stand on set and watch over the shoulder of my camera operator. The temptation, if you're on set of course, is to just watch the performance live instead of viewing it through the viewfinder or on the monitor. That, however, doesn't really show you the performance that will be seen by the audience. That is the key. You need to see what the audience will see. But I like to actually 'feel' the performance as well, which is why I want to be right there with the actors.

Director of Photography (DP, Cinematographer):

The person in charge of what gets filmed—what the cameras actually record. This is the person who sets up the shots. They know all the different cameras, what they are and aren't capable of doing. They know lighting, framing, shot composition and how all of this relates to storytelling. They are in charge of the entire camera crew, including ACs (assistant camera—the camera operators), focus pullers, loaders, the grips and gaffers, best boy—everyone who will impact the image.

This person works closely with the director to create a shot list and often works from a storyboard created by the director. The DP is another position that is often part of the director's team. If the director has a DP they like working with, hire that person. If not, or if the director's DP is unavailable, then you and the director will spend time looking at reels to choose a DP that will best suit the genre, style and look that the director is trying to achieve. This person should be brought into the production early in pre-production in order to help select locations, camera equipment and lighting and plan shot lists and shooting schedules.

NOTE: a word about DPs who own their own equipment. This may seem like a great time- and money-saver. Basically you're hiring a guy who owns his own camera and comes with it so you're getting a 2 for 1. Not bad. I'm not recommending against this, but I have been advised by many of my director friends that they've hired DPs who 'own their own equipment' but *don't actually know how to use it.* Yeah, you read that right. Some of them just bought a fancy camera, advertised themselves as having it (and charged more for their services because of that fact) and you're their guinea pig. This has never happened to me because my DP doesn't own a camera—his philosophy is that equipment is changing and being upgraded so regularly that it doesn't make sense to actually buy anything. So we rent. So, a word to the wise. If you're going to hire someone who owns his own camera, be sure they know how to use it!

Gaffer/Best Boy:

These are the on-set electricians and lighting people. They work with the DP to light the set. Their job is actually to *control* light. Meaning how much/how little. They know how to light the set and get the DP exactly what he/she wants and which lights to use to get it (although the DP often will ask for *exactly* the specific light they want). But they don't always just set up the lights. They also set up the flags, the filters, the silks, the scrims—everything that has anything to do with light—or the absence of light—on a set. The gaffer and best boy are often part of the DP's team, and if they have people they like working with, hire them. Generally the DP has their own people (gaffers, best boy and grips) that they like working with. Again, we're talking about a well-oiled machine here.

Grips:

These guys move stuff around. They're the muscle of the set. They move the camera, the lights and the set pieces. If the camera is on a dolly on rails, they're often tasked to put it there and then move it when the time comes. They move lights around. They also move set pieces, if necessary.

Sound Mixer (Sound Guy/Gal):

One or more guys/gals who record all the sound on the set. He or she has a variety of equipment including a recording device, a mixer, one or more boom poles, microphones of various sizes—some of which attach to the boom and some of which are wireless and attach directly to the actors themselves. They'll ask for quiet at various times when they need it and record things you might think are unnecessary (room tone, anyone?). But just you wait…a good sound person is worth their weight in gold. Even if you're not paying anyone else—this is someone you should pay!! Their equipment—which they usually own themselves—costs a decent amount of money and good sound is very, very, very important. You won't get it recording from the camera mics. Don't even consider it. And if you think you can fix it in post? Forget about it! There are only two ways to fix sound in post: ADR (Automated Dialogue Replacement or looping) the entire film or have your editor or sound designer try and filter out the offending noise. Both of those solutions are very time consuming and expensive! Nope, this is one person you'll definitely need.

You won't need to hire a sound person until a week or two before production. Make sure you don't wait until the last minute because you definitely want your first choice to be available and not on another shoot. How do you choose? Well, you can't really listen to a reel or anything because what are they going to do—play you bad sound? Okay, so you interview them, look at their credits on IMDb to see what else they've done, ask them what some of their biggest challenges as far as recording sound have been and what their solutions were. That ought to give you a good idea of how creative they are. Get a sense of whether this is someone you want to have around you, on set, for up to 14 hours. Oh, and survey your web of trust—there's got to be somebody out there who will recommend a good sound person.

Boom Operator:

This is the person who holds the microphone on a big, long stick, pointing it at the actor who is speaking and then turning it and pointing it at the other actor when they start to speak. The boom operator is connected to the sound person by way of a microphone cord, which attaches his microphone to the recording device or mixer. Sometimes the boom operator and the sound person are one and the same, and one person *can* do both jobs, if they're skilled and experienced. It is a way to save money if you can find someone who can do both jobs *well*. Don't think that all this person does is hold a stick and you can enlist an extra—or grip or PA—to do that on the day of the shoot. A good boom operator knows where to point the mic to get clean sound, how to keep the mic and the boom out of the shot and understands that even the slightest movement of his finger on the boom will be heard and picked up by the mic. Oh, and they've developed really, really strong shoulder muscles in order to hold their arms steady during the take. If the sound person needs a separate boom person, they'll usually have someone they like working with.

Production Designer (Creative Director, Art Director, Set Designer, Set Decorator, Set Dresser, Prop Master):

The production designer (and team) is in charge of the overall look and feel of the project in terms of what the sets and locations will look like. Their team is in charge of the various props, designing them or obtaining them, the procuring (or designing) of the set pieces and, ultimately, dressing the set. These people work with scripty to make sure that continuity is maintained on each set—the set pieces are properly placed and the props are put back if moved during filming. They also take care of the props. A good production designer has relationships at prop houses, furniture stores and rental houses and is very creative when it comes to designing and putting a set together, particularly those that take place in the future, the past or are in a Sci Fi or fantasy genre. They have a knack for interior design and, really, are artists when it comes to creating an atmosphere with furniture, props, set pieces and set decoration. They know that color and design will contribute to the overall emotional impact and will work with the director to establish a mood for each individual scene as well as the overall piece. If your piece is in a Sci Fi or fantasy genre and you're shooting in front of a green screen, they may work very closely with whomever is supervising your CGI (computer graphics imaging).

If you're on a very low budget one person may take on *all* these jobs and it may be YOU. A production designer will need to come on the project fairly early. Definitely at the start of pre-production, if not before. They need to see all the locations where they will take lots of pictures. They also need to meet with the director in order to get a sense of the mood and style of each scene, as well as find out what the tone and color palette is and start putting together a list of all the props needed. It can be a big job and you want to be sure to give them plenty of time to do everything. How do you find a good one? Most of them have books or a website—pictures of sets they've designed for other projects. Look at those. Listen to them talk about the projects they've worked on. What is their enthusiasm level? Is this someone who will be passionate about your project? Is this someone who shares the same vision as you and/or your director? If so, it will probably be a good fit.

Costume Designer (Wardrobe, Wardrobe Supervisor):

On a bigger budget project these actually may be two different people, but on a smaller budget it will probably be the same person. This person usually researches the type of clothing worn in the specific time period of your piece, if you're doing a period piece. They design costumes and obtain them. Sometimes they'll 'shop' from the closets of the actors and decide what will work for each scene. They can arrange for rental of costumes from a costume shop or donation of specific items (for credit in the film if they're a good negotiator) from a rental shop—like a tux rental store, for instance. This person works with the director to establish a look and color palette for each scene, knowing that colors and styles each play an important part in the subliminal emotional impact that is created in the frame. They then maintain continuity with scripty during the actual shoot. They are also responsible for cleaning and pressing all the wardrobe items and even designing and sewing specific items, if they're not available for rent. They generally have relationships at the various costume rental houses in town, as well as a broad knowledge of the resale shops and fabric stores. Oh, and they're also very handy with a sewing machine, glue gun, gaffer's tape and can usually design and whip up a costume in a matter of hours.

On one of my last films I needed several people to show up at a raid wearing FBI windbreakers and it turned out the local costume rental shop was out of them. So, at the last minute my wardrobe gal bought a bunch of black windbreakers and whipped up the FBI monikers on the backs—they looked just like the real thing. She did all of them in an afternoon.. My most recent project was a period piece from the 1930s. That same wardrobe gal was thrilled as she had just wardrobed a theatre piece from the '30s and still had all the costumes. This is what a good wardrobe person will do—they'll have a closet full of different costumes from different time periods.

Your wardrobe person will also want to come in at the beginning of pre-production. Depending upon how specific the wardrobe requirements are, maybe even earlier. If it's a period piece and the period is a difficult one, you might want to give them more time. If it's set in the present, then they won't need nearly as much time. If you're asking them to sew/create costume pieces for any of your actors, you have to give them enough time to do that. How do you find a good one? Most of them have books, with pictures of things they've done in the past, which will give you a sense of their expertise.

Hair and Makeup:

On a bigger budget project these jobs are separate, but on lower budget projects they'll be lumped together. This person does the hair and makeup of the actors. All the actors. Or, if you've made specific arrangements with your hair and makeup person, just the principal actors. If that's the case, you have your extras and day players show up 'camera ready' (meaning hair done and made-up, ready to go). Their responsibility is to put camera-ready makeup on the actors, provide a period-appropriate hairstyle (and know what that is) and then be on-set to make sure that it stays looking good and provide last looks before each shot (meaning look at the actor to be sure they don't need a touch-up and, if they do, give them one).

The makeup skills required are far more than just owning the product. Having the education to know how color behaves under different light temperatures can save you headaches in post. Expertise in prosthetics is also valuable in a makeup artist's skill set. This includes more than just applying blood and blood effects. It means knowing how to control the spatter and cleaning it up at your location. Otherwise, be prepared to pay a cleaning penalty. Your hair and makeup can be hired a week or two before production begins, unless you have specialized prosthetics that require fittings in advance or anything that requires testing in advance. They, too, should have books or online websites to show off their previous work and are usually proud to talk about where they've trained. Make sure your makeup artist has trained with one of the recognized schools and if you need bruises or cuts and scrapes or anything other than just beauty makeup, look closely at what they've done before.

Second Assistant Director (2nd AD):

Again, this is not an assistant to the director. Not technically an assistant to the First AD, either, although the Second often acts as the 'right hand man' to the First. The First and Second do coordinate the shooting schedule together. Basically the Second handles all the paperwork on the set, and getting people TO the set: Call sheets, production reports, SAG/AFTRA contracts, etc. This person gets the preliminary call sheets out, in advance, and makes sure that tomorrow's final call sheet is in everybody's in-box before the end of the day today. This is the person who coordinates with the actors to let them know when they're working, what their call time is and makes sure they know how to get to the location/set.

This person is also responsible for getting talent from holding to the set and back. This person often orchestrates or "directs" the background talent during takes where they are visible in the frame, as well. On a low budget project this position is almost always taken over by the First (or a really good PA in terms of wrangling talent and the director in terms of directing the background talent). This person can be hired right before production begins and, again, often the First knows and can recommend someone for this position.

Production Assistant (PA):

These are the people who seem like they're at the bottom of the totem pole and yet they are vitally important to every production. Without PAs you really couldn't get most projects through production. They do *everything*. Anything and everything that doesn't fit in the above descriptions that needs to be done—they do. They are often running errands, picking up things and people—last-minute stuff, without which the project would grind to a halt. They are there to assist, literally, you, the producer, the director and the production in any and every aspect. Whatever desperately needs to be done—they do. Hire as many of them as you can and pay them what you can—you won't be sorry.

These people can, and should, be hired both at the start of pre-production (in order to help you during that phase) and at the beginning of production (to help you during that phase), if possible. How do you find a good one? Any way you can. Very often people know people who have worked in this position on past projects and can recommend them.

Craft Services (Catering, Crafty):

This person or team is responsible for providing the meals and snacks during the production. The technical term for the snacks provided throughout the day is craft services (crafty) and the technical term for the lunch or dinner that you break production to eat is catering. On a bigger budget project these two are provided by different companies. On a lower budget project it will be one person, or team, who provides it all. This is a VERY IMPORTANT part of your production. Please devote a decent portion of your budget to this. Especially if people are working for nothing—or next to nothing—you should show them how much you appreciate them by feeding them well. People will be much more willing to work hard for you—and will feel much better about doing so—when they are well fed. Don't just order a pizza or sandwiches from Subway. That is lame! Actually get someone to cook a hot meal for the cast and crew. It will make all the difference in the world. Also, have water on hand—and some sodas. Don't forget the snacks—good snacks—not just twizzlers.

On my productions we have *great* crafty and great catering and we are legendary for it. That's why my crews come back and work for me over and over again, even when I have to do some very low budget stuff. They know they're going to eat so much better on my set than they would if they were sitting at home and, hey, they're going to have some fun, too! Also, a good crafty and caterer will be sensitive to dietary restrictions of the various cast and crew and adaptable on the fly when your carnivores consume all of the veggie lasagna— meaning you have to create something quickly for your vegetarians. Be aware that these days healthy options are a key component—on my last shoot no one, and I mean NO ONE ate the sweets, candy, twizzlers and sodas. Everyone wanted the coconut water, grilled veggies, trail mix - healthy food. This person or people can be hired a week or so before production. Give them time to do some shopping and preparation before your production begins. If you hire them the day before production begins you aren't really going to have great food because you haven't given them enough time to go shopping. You'll want to get recommendations from other producers/directors who have done their own indie productions—who did they use—and love—for their craft services?

Casting Director (CD):

The casting director is involved in bringing you choices for the various roles in the project. She does the work of going through mountains of submissions for each role, narrowing the field down to a manageable number (say 4-6 per role) and then bringing those actors in to read for the director (and you). If preferable, the CD can have a larger number of actors read for each role, putting them on tape (or having the actors put themselves on tape) so that the director (and you) can watch them in the comfort of your own home or office and narrow the choices down to the few that you want to see in person. Or, if you prefer, you can never see the actors in person, preferring only to watch the taped submissions.

The casting director is in a unique position of having worked with many actors and their representatives over the years and so has relationships with people, often at a higher tier than you, and can suggest people that you don't often take into account or don't think would consider doing a lower budget project. The Casting Director also knows all the various contracts and has the ability to negotiate with talent representatives in your stead. Once you have the budget to afford to hire one, it's definitely worth your money to do so. There are many CDs out there who work as assistants in bigger offices who would love to take on your smaller-budget indie project to get some more credits on their own. The casting director will come into the project fairly early in the process. As soon as you have a script and a director and you've got your money in hand and budgeted out, you'll want to sit down with the director and casting director and talk about who you see in the various roles and when you might want to post a breakdown and have sessions. Depending upon when your start of production is scheduled, that could happen right away or a few months down the road. How do you find a good one? I'm not sure there are any really bad ones out there. I think it's really just a matter of finding someone you and your director click with, who is also excited about the project.

Post-Production Supervisor:

This person's job is to coordinate the scheduling, execution, adherence to deadlines, budget and workflow of the project through the post-production process. This includes editing, sound editing and foley, music, cgi (if necessary), color correction/grading (if necessary), sound/dub mix and output for final deliverables (film, dcp, blu-ray/dvd, etc.). Believe it or not, I think you should hire your post-production supervisor *before* you start production. Whaaa???? Yes. If you do, you'll save yourself a mountain of headaches in post. If you don't, well then don't blame me if you spend twice as much as you need to in post-production. Why? Because this person can help you, your DP and your editor coordinate your workflow.

What exactly is workflow? It's how your DP is going to acquire the footage (shoot it) and how the editor is going to ingest and, ultimately, cut it together (edit it). All that requires knowing how the editor works, what system they prefer using, how fast their computer is, and what type of camera the DP wants to use. If *all* of that information is known, up front, by the post-production supervisor, then they can alleviate all sorts of problems that can arise in post from incompatibilities between this editing system and that camera, this computer system (which isn't fast enough) and that camera (which shoots 4k), etc. Sometimes your post-production supervisor is also your editor—if they are really knowledgeable. However, these people are few and far between. How do you find a good one? Talk to people—especially people who are involved in post-production, i.e., editors, sound editors, composers and the like. See who they like to work with.

Editor (Colorist):

This person cuts the raw footage, first into a rough cut and then into the final, finished product. These days it generally starts with ingesting the footage into their computer from the digital media and syncing the dailies. This can be done by an assistant editor, but on a lower budget project is often just done by the editor themselves. Once there is a rough cut the director and editor will refine the cut to achieve a locked picture—the final cut. It is rare that any other post-production activities can happen before picture is locked. Once picture is locked your color correction can start. On a bigger budget project this is done by a separate person who is a specialist in color. However, on a lower budget project your editor can usually handle the tweaking of the color and exposure of the various scenes that need it.

I think it's a good idea to have your editor picked out before you start production, especially if you don't have a post-production supervisor. This way your editor can advise you regarding work flow and help save you time and money in post by working with your director and DP, figuring out the most cost-effective way to shoot and acquire your footage. I know many, many producers who have waited until their film was shot to hire an editor and have found out, only too late, that they could've done things just slightly differently when they shot their project, which would've made his job easier, less time consuming and, therefore, less costly.

How do you select a good one? This is tricky, to say the least. Not everyone with a computer and an editing system is a good editor. Not everyone who has mastered their editing system, be it FCP, Avid, Premiere or whatever, is necessarily a good editor, either. Editing is a skill that requires a good eye, ear and rhythmic sense. Your editor has to understand the different genres—or at least the genre *you've* shot in—and how to cut to that genre, because different genres require a different rhythm and pace. Also, the less experienced your director, the more experienced your editor had better be. Talk to people. Get recommendations. Look at their work. Get a sense of the different types of work that they have cut. Do they specialize? In your genre? Have they ever cut using the format you're shooting? Find out.

Sound Designer (Foley Editor):

The sound designer/foley editor adds ambient sound, environmental sounds, special fx, sound fx and foley to the locked picture. In many cases they will be replacing production sound with an enhanced sound design. Why do you need this, you ask. "We got good sound and paid for it, didn't we?" Well, yes and no. You got good, clean dialogue, yes? But the microphone wasn't down on the ground, picking up the footsteps as your actors walked into the room. Nor was it over by the door recording the squeaking hinge. You didn't really have that telephone ring, did you? No. These sounds need to be added in post. This is the guy who does it.

Foley (the recording of footsteps, body hits, gunshots, etc.) may be generated from an online library or created by a foley artist on a foley stage. In either event, you need to have these various sounds in your film in order for it to sound real and professional to the viewing audience. You won't be able to give the project to your sound editor until you have a locked picture. You can certainly spend the time that your editor is working on the film interviewing people and finding a good sound editor, but they won't be able to actually do any work until the picture is locked. Often your editor or post supervisor will have recommendations for this person. I even had my composer recommend someone to me who is now a permanent part of my team.

Composer (Orchestrator, Music Supervisor):

This person will watch the locked picture and create music that enhances the emotional impact of your story. If you have a director who knows music—or knows what they want—they'll surely have input in this area. If you know music you'll want to have input here. This can be an area of great artistic collaboration. An excellent score can make a good movie great. A so-so score can make a great movie just okay. A good composer will know where to put music and where to leave music out, knowing that the absence of music (silence) can be as powerful as the music itself.

You should also know that there is the option of buying royalty-free music online and scoring the piece in this way. The plus side of doing that is possibly getting your music for less than hiring a composer. The downside of that is getting cookie-cutter music that doesn't fit your piece like a glove. Many films today use a music supervisor who seeks out popular or 'underground' music for placement in your film. Know that any copyrighted music will require appropriate clearances that match your distribution plan. Failure to secure complete clearances in advance may prevent you from negotiating any kind of distribution, foreign or domestic, or even film festival exhibition.

On bigger budget projects, the composer writes the main musical thematic material and the orchestrator orchestrates it—meaning the orchestrator decides which instruments are going to play which parts of the melody. On a smaller budget project your orchestration will be created by your composer and will often be done completely electronically, meaning in the computer. However, live musicians may be used in conjunction with an electronic score. If you are working with any kind of live musicians you'll need to do a music mix.

The composer will not be able to start working on the project until you have a locked picture. Again, you can certainly start listening to different composers' CDs and make a selection of the person you want to work with while you're in the post-production process. Selecting a composer is a process that your director will be primarily involved in, but they may want you to weigh in as well. Look for someone who has done music in the style that you want for your movie, i.e., if your movie is a comedy and you want something light and fun make sure they have done music that is light and fun. Does the instrumentation of the music they've written sound funny to you? Remember what I said earlier—the music will help set the tone, so if the instrumentation doesn't help you 'feel the funny', move on to the next one.

You'll also want to be sure that the composer you select is able to be flexible—meaning they can take notes from the director (or you) and adjust accordingly. Some composers are less able to do this. I'm not sure why, but I have a theory. I believe it's the "I have a computer, I have a computer program so I'm a _____ (insert title here) syndrome." I find a lot of creatives fall into this subcategory, whether they be editors, composers, colorists or whatever. They have the equipment but don't really have the time, training or expertise with it. Choose wisely.

Sound Mixer (Dub Mixer):

This is the person who takes all of the sound

elements—dialogue, sound effects, ambience and music—and shapes them to create an aesthetically pleasing final output. This may include a multi-channel 5.1 surround sound mix or it may just be a stereo mix. Whatever the final output, this is what the audience will hear and it will determine how they feel about the project and whether they enjoy it, so this is of utmost importance. These people have awesome ears. They can hear things the average person can't hear. This will be the last person you hire. They won't come into the project until you have music and foley and a locked picture and you're almost done. Yay! But this is one of the most important people. They have to have some of the best ears in the business. They have to be able to hear things you and I can't. So how do you find this person? I got mine by recommendation. Note that your sound editor *probably* won't be your sound mixer. These guys specialize and usually only do one thing—not everything. So you'll want to find someone who specializes in mixing sound because these are the guys with the ears. They hear the tiniest little things and will be able to mix your soundtrack so it's clean and smooth and the relative levels of ambience, sound fx, foley, dialogue and music all sound *just right* relative to each other.

CGI Specialist:

Most low-budget projects don't actually need CGI (Computer Generated Images), but I throw this in here in the rare instance that yours does. One of the last projects I did, in fact the last *two* projects I did, needed CGI. Here, my editor (who was also my post production supervisor) helped me find a student, who was working on getting his college degree in film production and I wound up with some pretty spectacular visual effects for a very low price. These guys know their computers—and love geeking out on this stuff—and for a little money and credit in a real Hollywood project (read: their name on IMDb), you can get some awesome stuff. Don't be afraid to ask.

II. Film Festival Information

Here is a list of the online submission platforms for film festivals. It is by no means exhaustive—just the ones that I have used and found fairly easy to navigate, understand and do research through. Be aware that new film festivals come along almost every year. So this information will be dated almost as soon as it's published. But, hey, at least it's a place to start.

Without a Box – http://www.withoutabox.com

Even though they will have gone out of business by the time this book is published I list them first. Why? They're the granddaddy of them all—the ones who started it all. A division of IMDb.com (owned by Amazon, by the way), they had thousands of film festivals listed there and were free to join. All you needed to do was fill out a form with your film's complete (as complete as possible) information. The more complete the information the better, as it became the information that populated the film's IMDb page once you started submitting to 'partner' festivals. Those were the festivals that were approved by IMDb. It used to be that a short film had to be vetted (and I mean *extremely* vetted) in order to get on IMDb, meaning it had to be accepted at an approved festival or *screen* at an approved venue in town or be reviewed by an *approved* publication in order to be placed on IMDb. And web series? Well, *if* they had been around back then they would *not* have been approved. But, WAB changed that and grew with the times. It got to the point that all you had to do was *submit* to one of the approved (or partner) festivals and, once they'd logged in your submission, your film's page just showed up on IMDb in a week or two. Awesome! That was *so much better* than when I started!! Nowadays it's even easier to get your short film on IMDb so this function is no longer necessary. Which I guess is a good thing now that they're out of business.

Film Freeway -- https://filmfreeway.com/

This platform has quickly become as big as WAB. It, too, is a conglomeration of film festivals, mostly in the U.S. Once again you enter your film's information and submit to the various festivals. Each festival determines its own submission procedure and fee. I have used this site, more and more now as WAB has gone by the wayside. It seems easy to use and I liked that I can link to my password-protected Vimeo (or Youtube) link instead of uploading my screener to their site, although you can do either. This site basically took the place of WAB.

Film Festival Platform – http://www.filmfestplatform.com

A platform for short films to enter international festivals. It's free to sign up and enter your film's information and then they send you reminders when different festivals are open for submissions. You go on the site to see if (a) your film fits the festival's criteria and (b) what the submission requirements are and how to submit.

Short Film Depot – http://www.shortfilmdepot.com

This is strictly for short films, natch, and primarily those in Europe and Asia although they also list some in South America and the African continent. It's free to register your film here and they send out reminders when the festivals are accepting submissions. You just want to be sure to read all the submission requirements to make sure your film fits as the foreign festivals can have quite different requirements than the American ones.

Reelport – http://www.reelport.com

This is also primarily for foreign festivals but they

handle features and shorts. I used the Short Film Depot more than I used Reelport, but I did use both portals and found them both fairly easy to navigate and use.

I'd also suggest, if you're on Twitter, following @festivalfocus, @futureshorts and @festivalalert to find out about more film festivals around the world and @filmfestlounge, which rates and reviews film festivals.

As a footnote, I'll tell you that when I entered the game of film festivals with my first film, the bible for everyone was Chris Gore's *Ultimate Film Festival Survival Guide*. I still have it on the shelf. I don't refer to it anymore. It's dated and there's much more information available online now than ever before. That said, if you found a used volume of this in a garage sale or at a used bookstore and wanted to buy it and peruse it—you'd find some of the information is still valid. But let me caution you: any book, guide or person who tells you they have the secret to getting your film into Sundance or any of the bigger fests is just selling you a load of spin. Nobody knows how to do that *for sure*. You can make the best film in the world, and I mean the *best* film, and still not be accepted to the film festival that's number one on your list simply because your film didn't fit any of the programs they curated for that year. There's no magic bullet. Yes, the better film you make the *more* film festivals you're likely to get into and the *more likely* you are to get into the festivals of interest to you.

As you do some research on these various sites you'll find that, more and more, there are many festivals out there that accept web series. So if this is a way you'd like to go with your web series then check it out.

Also, as a side note, Moviemaker Magazine publishes their list of the 50 Coolest Film Festivals every year. It's interesting to look at, but again be aware that those kinds of lists are other peoples' opinions—not necessarily what's going to be best for *your* film. The same is true with asking your friends' opinions and other filmmakers' opinions. They can tell you about their experience, but their experience will not be the same as yours because their film is not the same as yours. Do your own research and make your own decisions about where you want to send your film. You might find that the little gem of a local festival in your own hometown turns out to be the best experience—one that yields better 'results' than any of the "A" festivals ever could.

Let me stress here...this is where those original two questions you asked yourself: "Why am I doing this?" and "What do I want to have happen because I did this?" come into play. Why did you make this project in the first place? What did you want to happen because you did it? One actor I consulted with wanted to take his short film out to some film festivals so he could meet other filmmakers in order to be considered as an actor for *their* future films. So, of course, his short film was going to feature him in a brand-specific role, but it also made sense for him to submit to *local* festivals that he could attend—going out of town wouldn't make much sense because only local filmmakers would be likely to hire him for their next project! Submitting his film and sending it out to screen at a festival in a different state seemed like a waste of money to him, given his original goal.

Along those same lines, I'd also like to acknowledge here that I have stressed in this book the benefits of creating your project using the highest standards and with the highest quality possible. Full disclosure: that is *my* brand. It may not *necessarily* be yours. Additionally, it may not necessarily be the answer to the two questions that I've asked you to pose. Let me explain:

I've had filmmakers come to me and say, "But Kathi, I've seen short films of less-than-stellar quality make it into Sundance," and I would have to admit that they are correct. I've seen that as well. So what's going on there? In those cases, I would have to say that it was the unique qualities of the story and the fact that it hit a home-run with regard to being something unusual, 'out-of-the-box' and right in line with what the Sundance programmers were looking for that year. If you've got a story that ticks *all* those boxes, and your goal is to get into Sundance, then I say go for it. But start with the two questions and then see where it takes you. Once you know the answers to those questions, it should become pretty clear what type of project you need to make.

III. Selected Reading

People frequently ask me what books I have read about the filmmaking process so I decided to add a section to this book with some of my favorites.

The following are some books that I have found to be particularly interesting and useful in various areas of production. I have no particular connection to any of the authors and receive no compensation whatsoever for recommending them.

Writing / Screenwriting
Any book by Syd Field, i.e., *Screenplay* or *The Screenwriter's Workbook*
Adventures in the Screen Trade and *Which Lie Did I Tell?* By William Goldman
Write It, Pitch It, Sell Your Screenplay by DMA, Donna Michelle Anderson
The Art of Dramatic Writing by Lajos Egri
Created By … by Steven Prigge
The First Time I Got Paid for It: Writers' Tales from the Hollywood Trenches by Peter Lefcourt, Laura J. Shapiro
Guide to Screenplay Structure by Dan O'Bannon
Save the Cat by Blake Snyder
The Writer's Journey: Mythic Structure for Writers by Christopher Vogler
Your Screenplay Sucks by William M. Akers

And probably the BEST way to learn screenwriting is to read screenplays. Go here to download some of the best:
http://gointothestory.blcklst.com/free-script-downloads/

Directing
Directors Tell the Story, Second Edition by Bethany Rooney, Mary Lou Belli
Kazan on Directing by Elia Kazan
Making Movies by Sidney Lumet
On Directing Film by David Mamet
Rebel Without a Crew by Robert Rodriguez
Something Like an Autobiography by Akira Kurosawa

And probably the BEST way to learn directing is to watch movies. Get a Netflix or Amazon Prime membership and have at it! Or rent the DVDs and listen to the director's commentary!

Producing
Chris Gore's Ultimate Film Festival Survival Guide by Chris Gore
Getting the Money by Jeremy Juuso
Hello, He Lied by Lynda Obst
Hope for Film: From the Frontline of the Independent Cinema Revolution by Ted Hope
Shooting to Kill by Christine Vachon

Casting
A Star Is Found: Our Adventures Casting Some of Hollywood's Biggest Movies by Janet Hirshenson and Jane Jenkins
The Star Machine by Jeanine Basinger (sort of fits this category, sort of doesn't)

Everything Else (Editing, Mindset, Philosophy, etc.)
The Big Leap: Conquer Your Hidden Fear and Take Life to the Next Level by Gay Hendricks
Brandwashed: Tricks Companies Use to Manipulate Our Minds and Persuade Us to Buy by Martin Lindstrom
The 8 Characters of Comedy by Scott Sedita
The Gifts of Imperfection: Let Go of Who You Think You're Supposed to Be and Embrace Who You Are by Brene Brown
Good In a Room by Stephanie Palmer

How Not to Make a Short Film: Secrets from a Sundance Programmer by Roberta Marie Munroe
In the Blink of an Eye: A Perspective on Film Editing by Walter Murch
Less: Accomplishing More by Doing Less by Marc Lesser
Self-Management for Actors by Bonnie Gillespie
The Slight Edge by Jeff Olson
The Tipping Point, Outliers, Blink by Malcolm Gladwell
Unsold TV Pilots: The Greatest Shows You Never Saw by Lee Goldberg
The War of Art, Do the Work, and *Turning Pro* by Steven Pressfield
Wishcraft: How to Get What You Really Want by Barbara Sher

IV. Sample Press Releases

In this chapter you will see three samples of press releases. You will note that they all have several things in common. First, they all have a title—a headline. The title or headline should be short, to the point and meant to grab attention. Somehow it should articulate a little something upon which the press release will expound in greater detail. It should also have at least one of the "PR buttons". Ahh, you ask, what *are* the PR buttons? They are sex, power, blood/death/harm, large sums of money, prestige, controversy.

Sex doesn't just mean that you are talking about the act itself, or something 'sexy'—it can also mean you mention "boy" babies or "girl" babies or, in the case of the press release about the web series, two *female* filmmakers who are bypassing "*male*-ruled Hollywood." (see how that works?)

Power refers to the wielding of influence over people, things, organizations or countries.

Blood/death/harm refers to the violence we so often see in the media. Or the threat of violence.

Large sums of money refer to either the money itself or things that are worth large sums of money, like jewelry, cars, sumptuous estates, private islands, etc.

Prestige can be had in the form of fame for fame's sake, or reputation and standing by virtue of having done something valuable to the community or the world.

Controversy is just that—conflict or something that antagonizes people…something that stirs them up.

The second element of your press release is the short statement. This immediately follows your headline and is a concise, one or two-sentence statement of the crux or main point of your article. It needs to be punchy and informative—you're letting people know exactly what the article is about in a sentence or two.

The third element of the press release is the body of the article. This is where you elaborate with all the details. I find it's fun here to quote various people involved in the project, including myself, as a device to draw people in. This is also where you can include links to specific locations you'd like people to visit (websites, the film festival screening schedule, for instance) and a photo. Your poster image can go here, or one of your 'behind the scenes' photos from the project, whichever you feel is a better representation of what you're describing in the article. If you're using PRLog, and you opt for the free press release, you will only be allowed one photograph. If you're using MaxIt Magazine, you'll want to check out their home page to see that the visual format they like is very different from a poster image. If you go with them you may want to re-size and re-imagine your poster artwork in order for it to look better on their website and in the follow-ups that they post there. They also allow more than one image and video, so you can post your trailer or behind-the-scenes footage.

Two Female Filmmakers Bypass Male-ruled Hollywood with Web Series "A Cup of Confusion"

Kathi Carey and Daniele Passantino have teamed to write and produce "A Cup of Confusion," a web series which follows a bright, young woman with big dreams. But she's getting conflicting advice from just about everyone -- a tale of the modern woman.

FOR IMMEDIATE RELEASE

PRLog (Press Release) - **Apr. 20, 2012** - Kathi Carey and Daniele Passantino have teamed to write and produce "A Cup of Confusion," a web series directed by Carey which follows a bright, young woman just out of college who has big dreams about what she wants to do with her life, but who's getting lots of conflicting advice from her friends, her older brother – everyone. It's a tale of the modern woman.

Userfox Email Solutions
Userfox.com/Email_Marketing
Sign Up For A Free 30 Day Trial.
Userfox Converts Free to Paid Users

AdChoices

"It's fun, funny and, we hope, will be a hit with young people everywhere who have hopes and dreams about their own futures but aren't quite sure about how to achieve them," says Daniele Passantino.

Carey and Passantino have lined up their first sponsor, Dave's Homeroast, a creator of home-roasted coffee beans, for the web soap and its first season of 4 episodes. It's a perfect pairing since the series is ultimately about the heroine opening a coffee shop.

ConfusionPR

"So many, entrepreneurial women in entertainment are turning to the Internet as an outlet for their creative expression," says Carey. "Creating web content is a way to reach an audience hungry for a vision and unique take on the world." Award winning filmmaker Kathi Carey and her collaborator Daniele Passantino are two such women. "A Cup of Confusion" is their contribution.

To see the trailer for the series visit http://www.cupofconfusion.com

Photo:
http://www.prlog.org/11855142/1

--- End ---

DEAD DROP Shakes Up the Cannes Film Festival

Described as "Fast-paced intrigue that leaves you wanting more" "Dead Drop," a cross between "The Usual Suspects" and "The Bourne Identity," is now screening at the Cannes Film Festival in the Short Film Corner.

FOR IMMEDIATE RELEASE

PRLog (Press Release) - **May 21, 2013 - SHERMAN OAKS, Calif.** -- "Dead Drop" was conceived and produced as proof of concept for a feature, now in development. It stars Golden-Globe nominee Brian McNamara and Basil Hoffman from last year's Academy-Award winning film "The Artist" and introduces Nick Liam Heaney, a former pro wakeboarder, X-Games Champion-top 10 in the World, who has turned his sights now to film. Says one reviewer, "Nick Liam Heaney is the next James Bond." Writer/Producer/Director Kathi Carey agrees. "I had no intention of making another short film," says Carey, "I had already done that quite successfully with my last short, "Worth."

The VA Home Loan
www.VeteransUnited.com
VA Home Loans - This is Our Focus. Pre-Qualify Online in 2 Minutes!

AdChoices

Indeed. Kathi's film "Worth" screened at 31 festivals and won 31 awards, was in the pool of short films to be nominated for an Academy Award in 2011 and is now available at IndieFlix. But, according to Kathi, "Nick can be very persuasive."

And that, according to another reviewer, can only be considered a good thing as, "Dead Drop is Aces!"

They are currently fielding investment offers for the feature. More information can be found at http://www.Carey-it-Off.com

Dead Drop

Photo:
http://www.prlog.org/12142001/1

--- End ---

31 Festivals Winner Worth Released To The Public

Category: News   Published Date   Hits: 617

Sherman Oaks, California, United States
Released
Short

Kathi Carey's award-winning film WORTH is now available for viewing by the general public on IndieFlix, Roku and Xbox.

Worth is a story about appreciating the potential that lies within everything while at the same time reminding us to NOT judge a book by its cover. Worth is also a film that Kathi never intended to make. Says Kathi, "I had already made a short film, "Reflections of a Life," taken it out on the festival circuit, won awards ... I felt like it was time to move on." But the Writer's Strike intervened. Kathi found herself out of work, along with the rest of Hollywood, for a period of weeks that dragged into months and she grew restless. "I always need to be working on something," says Kathi, "so I pulled this script out of the drawer, figured I could shoot it in a day and thought, 'why not?'"

Once Worth hit the festival circuit critics and audiences alike were unanimous in their praise. Said David E. Carter of the EMPixx Awards organization, "It was a pleasure to see this work. Everyone who saw it was greatly impressed. More than one viewer said, 'Gave me goosebumps.'" Another reviewer remarked, "I was profoundly moved by Kathi's film. I came to the screening as a blank slate but left reminded of the real power great filmmakers have to educate and inspire, as well as entertain. "Worth is a powerful film that should be seen by everyone." And NY Times critic John Anderson said "Truth is beauty ... Beauty-truth. WORTH follows that dictum. It is also a clever way of showing us how our perceptions can be rather twisted. The film ultimately screened at 31 festivals and won 31 awards.

To see the trailer & complete film: http://indieflix.com/indie-films/worth-34725/

Twitter: WorthMovie
Facebook: Worththemovie
http://www.facebook.com/pages/Kathi-Carey/43902504950
http://twitter.com/kathicarey
http://www.worththemovie.com

WORTH

Sid Page and Kathi Carey

The final press release is one of the first ones I wrote. You'll note that it's 'old school, meaning before the days of putting out press releases primarily on internet websites devoted to publishing and promoting your press releases. This was one I created and sent out to promote my first film at one of the festivals where it screened. You'll see that it doesn't *quite* follow the format that I've evolved into, with headline, opening paragraph and body of information, but it does have PR buttons, a headline and the body. It was still effective.

Today I use a combination of the internet websites PRLog, PRWeb and MaxIt (and others as I discover them) to post and publish my press releases. I also would not hesitate to send a press release to the various local outlets covering a film festival the next time I'm in the process of putting a film on the festival circuit. I think working that combination is a better way to get your message out there and make sure it actually gets to the people you want to know about your film.

However, that said, I would probably stick to the sites like PRLog and MaxIt for my publicity for something like a web series or if I launched a Youtube channel. It seems more appropriate, somehow, to promote your new media product…online.

FOR IMMEDIATE RELEASE
May 8, 2006
PRESS RELEASE: ALL MEDIA

CONTACT: David Manship
Carey-it-Off Enterprises

- Between 1947 and 1992 the San Francisco Bay Area had the highest reported rate of breast cancer in the world
- The number of new breast cancer cases in Marin County is 40% higher than the National average

Former Bay Area Resident Wins Best Drama at San Francisco Festival

Kathi Carey grew up in the shadow of Stanford University, but always dreamed of being an actress. She has returned to the Bay Area with her short film, "Reflections of a Life," and received the "Best Drama" award at the San Francisco Women's Film Festival. Written and directed by Kathi, "Reflections of a Life" is a love story about a woman who has seen her share of heartache only to discover she has breast cancer. The film explores how that affects her relationships with her friends, family and lover. The film is dedicated to the memory of Lenore Bateman, Ms. Carey's aunt who was also a Bay Area resident, who was diagnosed with breast cancer at the age of 51 and succumbed to the disease at the age of 63. Miss Carey also stars in the film, alongside Linda Gray (from "Dallas") and Fredric Lane (from "Lost"). The film has been recognized for its extraordinary original music and exceptional filmmaking craft. This award marks the second award as best drama in the space of 10 days.

In addition to the award at the SFWFF, the film has already won the Gold Medal Jury Award for Artistic Excellence from the Park City Film Music Festival and the "Gold" Special Jury Remi Award for Best Original Dramatic Short from Worldfest, Houston undoubtedly because everyone who sees it is so moved by the compelling story, the stunning visual look and acting that is on a par with any major studio release.

The film has begun to receive attention from journalists and media reporters across the country which has included appearances by Kathi on "The Screening Room," film producer Jonathan Krane's series out of Palm Beach, Florida promoting up-and-coming filmmakers, "Video-I" in San Jose, California a PBS series promoting independent filmmakers and the trailer being screened by ABC-7 news in San Francisco promoting the festival and "What's Hot in San Francisco." The film has also begun drawing the attention of breast cancer support groups and organizations interested in promoting breast cancer awareness.

V. Glossary of Terms

This is by no means comprehensive. But these are some common terms that may be unfamiliar to you, if you haven't worked a lot *or* produced much.

Aspect Ratio – The comparison of the width to the height of the frame of the film (or picture, if you're shooting digitally).

Apple Box – (*half apple, quarter apple*, etc.). Used to raise actors or an object to the correct height for the shot.

Available Light – Filming without the addition of any artificial light.

Back Light – Lighting toward the camera (shielded so it won't shine into the lens). Often used to create a silhouette effect.

'Back to One' – A phrase used to tell the actors to go back to the beginning of the scene, to their first marks, to begin again.

Best Boy – Gaffer's or Key Grip's assistant.

Call – The time that an individual member of the cast or crew is expected on set, usually listed on the Call Sheet.

Cans – earphones for the sound man (and others).

C Stand – Used to hold the various flags necessary to reduce the intensity of light or block certain portions of the light completely. Can also be used to hold or support other effects related to lighting like branches, leaves, etc.

"Cheat the Look" – A direction to the actor to move his face or eyes in such a way that the camera can see more of him than his 'natural' position would allow.

"Clean Entrance" – A direction to the actor that neither he nor his shadow should be visible to the camera before he makes his entrance to the scene.

Day for Night – A scene that takes place at night but is filmed during the day—usually for scheduling or economic reasons. If it is being shot outdoors, a special filter will be placed on the camera for the effect. If it is indoors, the windows will be blacked out.

Depth of Focus – The area within which objects placed at various distances in front of the lens remain in sharp focus.

'First Team' – The actors who will be doing the scene in front of the camera, as opposed to their stand-ins.

'Give Me a Level' – A request to the actors from the sound mixer to give him a sample of the dialogue—how loudly or softly they will speak their lines in the scene.

Half Load – The quantity of powder placed in the shell of a blank cartridge.

Hand Cue – Usually given by the director or assistant director to indicate the moment the actor is to enter the scene or to cue a specific piece of action.

Honey Wagon – Portable bathrooms used on location.

Hot Set – A set that is fully furnished and decorated (dressed) for shooting. Nothing on the set should be moved or touched except by the actors *during* the shooting of the scene.

Meal Penalty – The additional sum of money which a production company is responsible for paying an actor when they have worked beyond the time from his first call-time to his first meal break that has been negotiated by his union.

'On a Bell' – The designation that everyone needs to be quiet on the set—no walking or talking—since a take is in progress.

P.O.V. – Point of View. A camera angle that shows what someone in the film is seeing.

Reverse (Reverse Angle) – The opposite camera angle of the one just completed, to show the other side of the picture.

I never dreamed my life would be so good.
— Lee Daniels' The Butler, 2013
Lee Daniels, dir.

END NOTES

i http://www.funnyordie.com
ii http://www.youtube.com
iii http://www.imdb.com/name/nm0573658/?ref_=tt_cl_t2
iv http://www.imdb.com/name/nm0388819/?ref_=tt_cl_t3

vii http://www.indiegogo.com
viii http://www.kickstarter.com

x http://en.wikipedia.org/wiki/Labor_Management_Relations_Act_of_1947
xi http://osa.sagaftra.org
xii http://www.koldcast.tv
xiii http://www.blip.tv
xiv http://www.prlog.org/
xv http://www.maxitmagazine.com

www.ingramcontent.com/pod-product-compliance
Lightning Source LLC
Chambersburg PA
CBHW070943230426
43666CB00011B/2543